SUNBURNED

MEMOIRS OF A NEWSPAPERMAN

SUNBURNED

MEMOIRS OF A NEWSPAPERMAN

BY

DOUGLAS CREIGHTON

Little, Brown and Company (Canada) Limited
Boston • London • Toronto

Canadian Cataloguing in Publication Data

Creighton, Douglas
    Sunburned: memoirs of a newspaperman

ISBN 0-316-16078-4

1. Creighton, Douglas. 2. Journalist - Canada - Biography. I. Title.

PN4913.C74A3 1993   070.92   C93-094538-7

Photos appear courtesy of the *Toronto Sun* archives.

Cover design: Falcom Design
Interior design and typesetting: Annabelle Stanley
Printed and bound in Canada by Best Gagné Printing Inc.

Little, Brown and Company (Canada) Limited
148 Yorkville Avenue, Toronto, Ontario

Table of Contents

To my wife, Marilyn, especially. Throughout the most difficult time of our lives, she was always with me, always for me.

To our daughters-in-law, Ann, Terry and Christine, and our sons, Scott, Bruce and Don. I don't know what we would have done without them.

To Lynn Carpenter and Annemarie Cimowsky, my assistants and my friends, who kept me writing.

To Jim McCallum, my immensely gifted legal advisor.

And to the staff, who without concern for the consequences which could occur, wrote wonderful things about me and organized a birthday farewell which we will never forget.

Because of this, most of our memories will remain rich and deep.

CHAPTER 1

What Are Friends For?

T hey came through my door, pausing to shut it, which I never do. So I immediately knew something serious was up.

Herb Solway is the senior partner in the law firm Goodman and Goodman. He is the chairman of the Sun's human resources committee and has been a director since we started publishing. Herb and I have been casual friends for almost forty years.

Ron Osborne succeeded Don Campbell as chief executive officer of Maclean Hunter in 1990 when Campbell became chairman. He joined the Sun board in 1985.

Maclean Hunter owns about sixty-two percent of the Sun's shares. However, they have been bound by a standstill agreement with the Sun which limits Maclean Hunter to two directors on the Sun board and gives a large degree of freedom to management.

It was put in place because Sun directors did not want to sell nor relinquish control when the original deal was made. The standstill also helped Maclean Hunter with the CRTC who were nervous of media cross ownership. The standstill explained how Maclean Hunter could operate in cities where they owned newspapers, radios and television stations. It was to last five years.

Maclean Hunter meticulously honoured that agreement until this incident. At various times over the years it had been extended. When it expires in 1994, it will have been in effect about twelve years.

My relationship with the Sun ended about thirty seconds after the door closed.

Osborne has carefully explained that he was acting only as a director of the Sun and as a member of the powerful human resources committee — not as president or director of Maclean Hunter. "We are going to make Godfrey the CEO now." Solway said. "This is the unanimous feeling of the board." If that was true, I thought, it meant that George Cohon, senior chairman of McDonald's and developer, Rudy Bratty, had voted to get rid of me, and so had Paul Godfrey and Trudy Eagan — two inside directors who were on the board because I recommended them. (I found out later that Paul and Trudy had not been included in the first vote.)

My wife Marilyn and I saw a lot of George and Susan Cohon, and had had dinner in the country with them four nights before I got axed. I had nominated him to the board.

Rudy was an original investor and thus had been on the board since day one. We travelled a great deal with them.

When this is over, I thought, the end of these friendships will likely appear to us as far more tragic than my forced retirement from the newspaper.

Since the final signing of my package, I've held brief meetings with Osborne, Godfrey, Cohon, Bratty and Lionel Schipper, an original board member who has since become chairman, all of whom stress the same point: "How do we make you a part of the Sun again? You are the Sun."

How I could be dusted one day and be told " I was the Sun" a few days later by the same people is beyond me. What was understood by me was the reaction of the staff, my friends and family and the readers. They were all heart-warmingly and unanimously supportive.

That was all to come, however. My two loyal assistants, Annemarie Cimowsky and Lynn Carpenter, were crying. Paul Godfrey was waiting outside my office, and I was phoning home. As I dialed, I decided that when I left the office in about fifteen minutes, I would never return. I haven't and won't.

Godfrey was ashen. He wanted me to know he wasn't involved and knew nothing about it. That couldn't be true, I thought, but he certainly looked like he'd been punched, and was vowing to do what he could.

Paul Beeston of the Blue Jays was also on the board at my request. I had the highest regard for him. "He's just what the Blue Jays need," I said at the time. Paul phoned me in Florida a few days after I had become history and said he had been asked by the board to help settle the termination document with me. I resisted because I had already asked Jim McCallum, a retired director of the Sun, to represent me.

Several weeks later when negotiations had faltered, I ran into Beeston at a cocktail party and said: "If you still have the mandate, we may be able to break this log jam."

"I'll find out and let you know," he said. "I'll be in touch with you tonight or tomorrow morning."

I haven't heard from him since.

Nor have I ever heard from Frank King, our western director, concerning my ouster.

Paul Godfrey and Trudy Eagan, both of whom I hired, promoted and nominated to the board, said that the outside directors told them nothing about the affair until the Sunday board meeting a few days after I was relieved of my duties.

I hope so because it hurts to think they wouldn't raise their voices on my behalf.

"My" company had been taken away from me when I was just over a year away from retirement. My retirement date had been agreed upon in a series of letters between Ron Osborne and myself in September 1992.

The letters arose out of a casual discussion I had with Ron Osborne in my office after a meeting. He told me he was working on a succession report for his board which he presented once a year.

I told him I'd been thinking of this and would update him prior to his meeting. That afternoon I wrote to Ron. In part, I said, "I will turn sixty-five on November 27, 1993 (God and directors willing, I wrote rather fatefully) ... I will resign both as chairman and CEO and chair my final meeting in the spring of 1994 (the annual shareholders' meeting) ... I would, with the board's acquiescence, remain a director of the Sun and Maclean Hunter until I reach seventy." Then I wrote, "One thing that will not change is that the constant review of all our products be maintained after I'm gone. My idea to perpetuate this, as I mentioned, would be to give Hartley Steward a title which clearly identifies him with the product and a seat on the board which would be a just reward for Hartley, having helped start four newspapers. This would also be an excellent message to the staff when they see that appointment. I know your aversion to staff people on the board, Ron, and up to a point, I agree, but this particular area means a lot and I hope that it would be considered. This appointment would not happen until the shareholders' meeting in 1994."

By beauty of fax, I received his reply the same day. "I agree that spring 1994 is the right time to step down as chairman and CEO. We are delighted you will remain on the Sun and Maclean Hunter boards until you are seventy."

I had said my personal staff had to be looked after and Ron wrote, "As far as Maclean Hunter is concerned, you need have no concerns about the way in which your personal staff will be looked after. Obviously, the experience of working with somebody like Doug Creighton is not something that can be replaced in an identical fashion, but within our combined operations, I would be astounded if we cannot find suitable challenges and fair rewards for everybody involved." Then he replied to my point about editorial focus.

Significant, in my mind anyway, is the fact that these letters were never shown to the other board members until after the deed was done.

◆ ◆ ◆

I wonder if any members of the board looked into a mirror and wondered what they would feel like if this happened to them? I warned Solway and Osborne that the board had not thought out staff and reader reaction. It turned out to be even larger than I thought it would be.

My family's and my plans for a gradual move towards retirement are dead, of course. And the swiftness and nature of the Maclean Hunter intervention has meant a dramatic end to important friendships and several directorships. I resigned from the Maclean Hunter and McDonald's boards shortly after. As I said, I rejected Ron Osborne's offer to stay on the boards of Maclean Hunter and the Sun. How could I?

I know that boards' service these days has become more of a challenge and a risk. But for the life of the Sun, our board worked hard. They helped us strategically and encouraged us to remain entrepreneurial. But boards also exist to help companies maintain a favourable corporate image. That, I think, has been hurt.

Several people over the years of the Sun have been kind enough to call me a forgiving man ... sometimes to a fault. I have really tried to avoid confrontation and to look for some way to avoid ending twenty years of personal and business success. I can't.

Our staff, in my view, was the hardest working, most involved, and happiest I've ever worked with. Now, I understand, morale is a problem. Some board members deny this, but I think all they need do is look at their faces.

Whatever the reason for my forced retirement as CEO, and God knows I'm no angel, I still can't understand how it could be handled this way. I'm truly sorry but I can't forgive.

Naturally there comes a time in these matters when both sides must get together to work out an agreement as satisfactory to both sides as possible. Negotiations, of course, are usually difficult and wind up limiting some of those involved in what they can say or do. The contents themselves are usually private.

Nonetheless their actions have made me a bit of a celebrity. I was waiting to cross Queen Street at lunch time when a streetcar stopped in the middle of the block. The front door opened and the driver waved a copy of the Sun at me. "Don't let the bastards get you down," he yelled.

Not much later my wife and I were walking to Maple Leaf Gardens for a play-off game between the St. Louis Blues and the Toronto Maple Leafs. We were moving quickly, having lingered at George Bigliardi's restaurant, (in my view, the best steakhouse in Toronto). Up ahead, a beggar with a loud voice was asking people for $1.25 so he could get something to eat. At that moment our eyes met. "You don't have to give me money," he shouted. "You're just like me — out of a job."

But life must go on. I've reminded my family that we have had twenty-one years at the Sun which did much to enhance our lifestyle as well as the lifestyles of our original investors. In addition, I had another twenty-two years at the old *Toronto Telegram* in the business I love.

I'm going to write about those forty-three years.

Hi Ho Silver

I t was 1949 and I had just ended my one-year career as a post boy at the Toronto Stock Exchange on one day's notice.

I was going to be a reporter at the *Toronto Telegram*, one of the country's major newspapers. I was twenty-one years old.

The paper was referred to as the "Old Lady of Melinda Street." It didn't take me long to figure out why. It acted like one. They gave me two streetcar tickets to go to the first bank hold-up I covered.

My benefactor was an American — Cap Hara — who was the Tely's advertising director and also a friend of my parents. Even more importantly, he knew the newsroom was looking for a suburban reporter. Cap got the job for me and immediately visited our home to give me the good news. I was out, and Cap and my father had a few libations — maybe more than a few.

When I arrived home, Cap, who was blind in one eye, had replaced his glass eye with one with the American flag in it. "Welcome to the newspaper business," he said. "You'll see lots much worse than this before you're through." He was right.

I knew it was different right from the start. For one thing, I made five dollars less a week than I had made changing numbers at the stock exchange.

It seems I had always wanted to be a journalist. There it was in the *Humberside Collegiate Yearbook* — "going to be a reporter," it said, although for the life of me, I can't remember that I told the reporter that.

The only previous connection our family had to journalism was my great-uncle David Creighton who, with a partner, worked in the composing room of the *Owen Sound Sun-Times*. He eventually purchased it and became publisher. Later he was elected as a Conservative member to the Ontario Legislature and then, with the help of Sir John A. MacDonald, became editor and publisher of the Globe for thirty years.

While working at the stock exchange, I worked part-time for the *Canadian High News*, a weekly paper aimed at high school students.

Stan Houston worked there as well. We became good friends and he moved to the big time a few weeks earlier than I did. He wound up covering the Maple Leafs before he moved on a few years later to public relations. He still runs his own firm.

There were five of us from High News who were offered jobs by the Telegram over a period of a few weeks. George McCullagh, a vibrant millionaire, had bought the Tely from its trustees and was endeavouring to inject some youthful opinions into a paper which had become a rather faceless product with no clear vision.

One guy who didn't take up McCullagh's offer was my High News deskmate John Aylesworth. Aylesworth and I wrote "Teen Talk" at High News and he was in training to begin the comedy team of Peppeatt and Aylesworth.

They achieved prominence when they made the *Ed Sullivan Show* and later became writers for Perry Como and other television stars.

John was an original. One day, as we were writing "Teen Talk", I saw him staring out the window. He was watching a guy and his secretary making love in the office across the square from us. Practically standing on his head to do it, Aylesworth got the fellow's name from his window. He was a lawyer and John phoned him.

We could see the secretary painfully get off her boss's knee to answer the phone. "Let me speak to Mr. so and so," John demanded.

"He's busy, he can't come to the phone," the secretary replied.

"He has to, I have to speak to him," Aylesworth pleaded.

Finally the lawyer relented and came to the phone. "This is God speaking. Aren't you ashamed of yourself?" thundered Aylesworth and hung up.

The lawyer was stunned and began looking around while telling his secretary what had happened. Finally, they saw the two of us bent over in laughter. He shook his fist at us, then darted out the door.

Aylesworth and I beat it out of our office, figuring that's where the lawyer was headed. We hid out in the Savarin Tavern on Bay Street for the rest of the afternoon.

When I started at the Tely, I was told I was to cover the Lakeshore, which included Mimico, New Toronto and Long Branch. But for the first few weeks, I was to write general news and learn about the paper.

The CNE was on that first year and I interviewed Gene
Autry and the Lone Ranger. Autry used his own name and
has become a very wealthy man. He now owns the California
Angels baseball team. The Lone Ranger was ... well, the
Lone Ranger. His real name was Clayton Moore but, according to Warner Brothers public relations man, Al Dubin, he
actually thought he *was* the Lone Ranger.

Al had some evidence. He had delivered his agenda to the
Royal York that morning. When the door opened, there was
the Lone Ranger wearing his pyjamas — and his mask.

Older readers might remember that the Lone Ranger neither drank nor would let people in his presence take a sip.
This led to dramatically shortened press conferences.

After the general press scrum, I talked briefly to him about
silver bullets, his horse Silver and his Indian guide, Tonto.
Then I mentioned his love life. "I have none," he replied
angrily. "The Lone Ranger doesn't have time for affairs," he
said, thus enabling me to write one of the worst lead para-
graphs of my career.

"The Lone Ranger is forty-two and never been kissed," I
typed. I thought such a character would contribute greatly
that evening to Celebrity Night at the Press Club. I asked him
to come, and gave him the club's and my phone numbers.

Then I phoned my wife Marilyn to tell her I would eat
downtown and meet her at the club. Since she had just finished cooking dinner, the phone call didn't leave her in the
best of humour.

About ten minutes later, the phone rang at home again.
"No, Doug is not in," she told the caller. "Is there any message?" she asked.

"Just tell him the Lone Ranger called," the voice said.

"This is not funny," Marilyn said and hung up on him.

The next day, I interviewed Autry. A couple of hours later, he fell off his horse in front of thousands at the CNE. I decided my journalistic future didn't lie with celebrity interviews.

♦ ♦ ♦

One's first by-line story is an important event to every fledgling journalist. My first one was on a story I wrote on the death of Duncan Bull, a prominent Conservative and Brampton cattle breeder. The story was okay, but the headline was not the sort that found its way into family scrapbooks. It said: "Bred Best Jerseys, Duncan Bull Dies."

I starred again a few months later. Marilyn's family's next door neighbour was a nice chap named Albert Virgin. He was a provincial government bureaucrat who had just been promoted. Marilyn's mother thought it would be a good idea to write a nice story about him. Naturally, we all thought it was a good idea. Once again, the story was fine but the headline read: "Change of Life for A Virgin."

I thought maybe I should buy the Lone Ranger's mask, as did Marilyn's mother.

♦ ♦ ♦

But it wasn't all fun and games in those early Telegram days. The business of getting it first and getting it right was no less frantic then.

One of the most nerve-wracking stories I worked on was Hurricane Hazel. I was a young reporter at the Tely when it hit Toronto.

Within a few minutes of midnight on Friday, October 15, 1955, rivers and creeks, normally quite quiet and serene, overflowed their banks and went on a rampage of unprece-dented destruction. The floods were exacerbated by the heav-iest rainfall and the strongest winds in Ontario's history. Before dawn hundreds of trees, bridges and buildings were uprooted.

The worst of Hurricane Hazel was over in six hours, but the damage it wrought could not be totalled for months or even years.

It left almost 100 people dead.

No one was prepared. Even the essential services treated the awful rush of water as routine until it was too late. Newspaper and radio warnings were meagre. When the 5:00 p.m. traffic rush began, heavy rain was falling, but again, people underestimated the power of the storm. It was simply taking a little longer to get home, they thought. Even later in the evening, police and fire spokesmen were still telling reporters they were in the middle of a quiet evening.

Then suddenly there was chaos. Lake Simcoe, swollen by the huge rainfall, burst through two dikes and swept through the rich black earth of the Holland Marsh. One policeman in a helicopter said it looked like a huge vegetable stew. The water flowed south towards a still largely unsuspecting Toronto.

And where was the Telegram's budding young reporter? In bed, fast asleep. But not for long.

I struggled out of a deep sleep to answer the phone. It was Doug Stuebing, the Tely's night city editor. "Go right to the Humber River where it's close to the Old Mill," he barked at me. "Five firemen drowned there when their fire engine got washed into the river."

"Doug," I said. "Stop taking your coffee breaks in the

Cork Room (a bar across the street from the paper). The Humber River isn't more than two feet deep there." I promptly hung up.

Stuebing called back quickly. He was not amused. I got the impression if I didn't get going quickly that it might be the last call I'd get from the Tely city desk. Ever.

I dressed, jumped into the car and started what should have been a five-minute drive. Dozens of cars littered Bloor Street, abandoned. People walked about aimlessly. After about twenty minutes of manoeuvring the car in and around people and debris, I saw the cause of the concern. The Humber, usually little more than a stream, had become a raging, unrecognizable giant of a river, overflowing its banks everywhere in the area.

It was estimated that 322,000,000 tons of water fell into the Humber watershed in that one day. During the storm, the Humber averaged over thirty feet deeper than its norm.

For its twenty mile stretch, the Humber clawed at its banks, determined to breach them. For a while, the town of Woodbridge was completely cut off. Six people died. At Thistletown, the Sick Children's Isolation Hospital was blacked out.

Still, the crest of the flood swept on. Not far south of Lawrence Avenue it struck its most staggering blow, on Raymore Drive.

As is often the case in tragedies on the scale of Hurricane Hazel, bizarre incidents are commonplace. This one happened about two hours after the swollen river raged through Raymore, uprooting seventeen houses and sweeping them away.

A policeman in a police cruiser stationed at the top of the street spotted a man wandering dazed down the ravaged street. He was obviously still tipsy from a night on the town.

"My house is gone," he told the dumbfounded officer. "My wife is gone and I can't find my friends.

"Help me look," he pleaded with the officer.

How he got to Raymore Street from downtown remains a mystery. Why the police cruiser happened to be at the top of the street when the man began to look for his house, his wife, and his friends also remains unexplained.

But that's how the police learned about seventeen missing houses and thirty more deaths by drowning.

Raymore Drive is off Scarlett Road in Toronto's west end. Scarlett Road runs alongside Lambton Golf Club, where I store my twenty-one handicap. There is a huge tall tree guarding the entrance to the fourth green which is across the Humber River.

The police and I found a man's body in the lower limbs of the tree, maybe twenty feet above the ground. "The poor guy climbs a tree and still gets nailed," I said.

"Not so," the officer replied. "He drowned and the river put him there, it was that high."

Before it rushed into Lake Ontario, the river played a final, bitter trick. It chewed away at Lakeshore Bridge, eating away the supports. When the waters finally subsided, the streetcar tracks were all that held the bridge together.

It was my first major story, and I was trying to figure out how I did. I knew I was off to a slow start with Doug Stuebing, but I did pick up pictures of those poor firemen. I think I had the Raymore Drive tragedy to myself for about an hour, but I couldn't find a phone that worked to call it in for some time. When the Star came out, we definitely looked better and I wondered if the brass would recognize this.

Nobody said a word or sent a note. I made a note to myself even way back then that if I ever got anywhere in this crazy business, I'd make sure to congratulate people who went the extra yard for exclusives.

◆ ◆ ◆

In July of 1960, Marilyn and the kids and I were heading for Port Elgin, a nice town on Lake Huron, where my family had summered since I was two years old. I was enjoying showing them the things I had learned at the same place and same age.

In my childhood days we all learned to play golf and ride horses, and we would drink all the buttermilk we wanted for five cents. Outdoor movies had just arrived in Port Elgin and we made full use of them.

Just as we pulled out of the driveway, we saw the postman down the street waving some mail he had for us. One letter caught my attention. It was on expensive paper and it came from Rome.

A few months before, I'd been on what is still affectionately called in our industry a "freeload." Alitalia was inaugurating service from Montreal to Rome. I went along with seven other journalists including McKenzie Porter, a British journalist who then worked for *Maclean's* magazine, but eventually became a stalwart of the Sun. He was doing a piece on Canadians in Rome. He told me he had a very tight deadline.

We both went to see the Pope at a semi-private audience at the Vatican, but we also saw the other sights of Rome. There were about thirty people at the audience and the Pope met each of us individually. Then, a photographer, dressed in tails (at

9:00 a.m.), stood on what looked like a priceless antique chair and shouted: "Hold it." He took a picture of all of us. To my amazement, it was delivered to my hotel, and I paid for it with American Express.

On the plane on the way home to Canada, there was a stop in London. McKenzie, after a half-dozen scotches, decided to get off to go and see his "Mommy in Manchester."

When I last saw him he was running down an airport corridor, chased by two elderly security officers who were no match for him.

A couple of weeks later, the late Borden Speers, editor of *Maclean's*, called me to say Porter was one day late for his story on Rome. "Do you know where McKenzie is?" he asked.

"Yes I do," I replied. "He's visiting his Mommy in Manchester." McKenzie's story appeared a month later.

The letter from Rome, I suspected, had something to do with that trip. I had decided with a full week there, I should write something for the paper. I had read a story in the *New York Times* about a Roman tailor who built models of world leaders and then tailored suits on the models and sent a second suit to the leader himself.

This caused small crowds to stop and look at Eisenhower, Nixon, *etc.* in their new free suits in the tailor's display windows. It increased business which escalated even more when a couple of the leaders came around while visiting Rome and actually bought suits and posed next to their figures right there in the windows.

I decided to look up the tailor. His name was Angelo Litrico and he was located on Via Sicilia, just around the corner from Rome's main drag, the Via Veneto. The last time I was in Rome he was still there.

He couldn't speak much English so we found an interpreter. I wrote the story and it appeared in the Telegram a few weeks later. I sent him a copy and promptly forgot about it.

Angelo didn't forget. This letter was from him.

Could I help, he wrote in a mix of fractured Italian and broken English. He had a brother, Agatino, who was coming through Canada to the United States to marry.

Canada was much the easier country to enter, he said, but alas he knew no one to sponsor him. So he used my name. He hoped I didn't mind. When I looked at the dates, I realized the ship had already docked. Agatino was somewhere in Canada.

I went back into the house to phone a casual friend, Max Steele, who had a lot to do with policing our immigration policies. Here I was sponsoring a guy into Canada and didn't know it, or him, and anyway, he was already here.

Max couldn't explain how that could happen, but he would check and let me know. Luckily, he made note of the call.

We carried on with our three weeks of holidays and, when we returned, there was a memo from Max. That week I had dinner with RCMP Inspector Woods Johnson. We casually discussed Agatino. Luckily, he also made a note to himself.

I guess we all forgot it again until the end of September when the tailor wrote to me again.

Agatino would be in Toronto with his wife-to-be, the letter said. His visa was expiring in a few days. His fiancée apparently was having trouble getting into the U.S.

"Thanking you in advance," Angelo concluded, "for all you might be able to do for my brother. Always at your disposal for all what you may need from me in Rome."

As if by magic, the brother and his bride-to-be showed up at the Tely a few days later. I phoned Max Steele and told them what they wanted and also that I didn't give a damn whether Agatino got the extra time in Canada or not. Anyway, they let him stay a little longer.

I'm not sure if I ever saw him again.

At the same time as all of this was transpiring, there was a battle going on in the Ontario Legislature concerning the depth to which organized crime had penetrated the province.

The Liberals got a leg up in the political fight in late summer when police in Toronto and New York combined to arrest several men in both cities. They claimed they had made the largest number of drug arrests ever made in Canada.

The leader, police charged, was Albert Ageucci, a Toronto baker. He appeared in New York court every couple of weeks for a remand, then would return to Toronto.

The major story wire service bell was ringing one Sunday as I arrived at work. Ageucci had baked his last loaf of bread. His burned body (he also had a couple of bullet holes in him) had been found in a field outside of Rochester.

There was a charred wallet nearby with the identification for Agatino Litrico along with a departure time for a cruise ship to Italy. Police in New York missed him by one hour. He and his wife-to-be were in international waters bound for Naples. Interpol would meet him. They were also interested in how he got into the U.S. They suspected it was through Canada. They wondered who might have arranged it.

I heard immediately from both my police friends wondering if I had had any further contact with the guy I sponsored into the country. No, I had not.

Furious, I phoned my friendly tailor in Italy. A voice came on the phone which I'm sure was Agatino's. He mumbled something about trunks with false bottoms and then the line went dead.

A New York detective, who went to Rome to try and get him back to the U.S., said he struck out in a sea of Italian bureaucracy and he finally returned empty-handed.

A couple of years later Marilyn and I stopped for a beer on the Via Sicilia. There across the road was Litrico the tailor's place. A cardboard model of JFK was in the window.

I went across and into the store. There was movement in the rear. I'm almost certain it was Agatino hurriedly whistling out the back door. Marilyn and I left, none the wiser.

If you're ever in downtown Rome on the Via Sicilia, drop into the little tailor shop. Feel free to use my name.

CHAPTER 3

The Police Beat

A lot of my friends in Toronto remember when we could walk almost anywhere in our city feeling confident of our safety. Robberies were something somebody else had, and not too often at that. We had maybe twenty or thirty bank robberies in a year.

Murders ran at roughly one-eighth the rate of killings in American cities of about the same size.

On the police beat, we used to summarize every house break-in. Now they're so numerous we don't even mention them unless there is a huge theft or a celebrity victim.

In my time on the police desk, I don't think I ever covered a bank hold-up in the city when the story didn't appear on page one, or at least within the first five pages. Now bank hold-ups are so numerous many of them don't even make the papers.

But violent crime is a huge worry, with assaults sometimes doubling the number the year before. Toronto isn't as safe anymore.

How did this happen to our city?

The tremendous influx of new citizens, literally from all over the world, has meant that our cities are no longer populated by lifelong residents. This tends to break down the strong sense of community that existed even up until a few years ago.

At the time I joined the Tely, the press as a whole tended to rely almost entirely on sources within the so-called establishment institutions.

A crime story rarely quoted anyone but police spokespeople. Economic stories relied on spokespeople from business, industry, or the Chamber of Commerce. Racial incidents were commented on by government or sources within the social service agencies.

One heard very little from minorities, the poor, or dissidents. But, in the 60's, the United States began to experience riots, student uprisings and war protests. Gradually newspapers, including those in Canada, began to report and, more importantly, to reflect, analyze and comment far more on these phenomenae. Now we've carried such coverage to the extreme.

Some view this coverage as anti-government and anti-establishment. I've always thought it was simply unfair.

The big problem, and to me disappointment, has been our inability to find representatives from these groups, and in a journalistic sense, train them so they could see both sides of the difficulties. Our efforts at the Tely came to nothing.

At the Sun, we had a little more success. We have a very good black reporter, Tom Godfrey, who has developed an introduction which helps. When he phones or knocks on a door for an interview, he says he's Paul Godfrey's brother. I advised Paul to get business cards printed saying he was Tom's brother.

It would be accurate to say that I think the reputation of both the media and the police has deteriorated badly. It would also be accurate to say that a lot of it is our own fault. We have a crisis in credibility. It's at the virus stage now, but if it gets much worse, it could become a full-blown health problem.

I admit that I have a pro-police bias and will never lose it. I have been an honourary member of the hold-up squad for years, my colleagues being Jocko Thomas of the *Toronto Star*, Ed Mirvish and Alan Lamport.

Unfortunately, at a time when they most need support, the police are hampered further by politicians and the economy. The economic squeeze and the decline in political will to tackle the problem has come just when we need two-person police cruisers and a return to the cop on the beat, along with the financing to do it.

As I mentioned, my first job with the Telegram was the police beat, covering the Lakeshore. The police and the press at that time had a relationship I would never see again. We were the good guys.

In those days, if you simply knocked on doors on Seventh Avenue looking for booze, you'd be unlucky if you had to knock on three doors before you found it.

There was little or no major crime, because the gamblers and book-makers would be after the guilty ones with as much energy as the cops.

There was a discreet room at the top of a Lakeshore hotel where the police and the press went most days or nights for a gratis meal and a few drinks.

One night, I was sitting with the police chief of Long Branch and New Toronto when the phone rang. It was the stone-faced part-timer who manned the phones at the New Toronto police station. He was also in charge of any prisoners, as the town's one cell was also in the station.

The chief's part-timer had bad news. He'd fallen asleep, and when he woke up his one prisoner, arrested for drunk driving, had pulled the bars open and left.

We started to rush to the station, but as we reached the ground floor of the hotel, there was the escapee — sitting at the bar downing a beer. We took him to the cell at Long Branch station. We hoped it had stronger bars.

◆ ◆ ◆

Fortunately, there are still some old-time policemen around. One of them, Toronto Chief Bill McCormack, remembers when the odds favoured the police.

He also knows that for the first time in Toronto, there is fear. Real or unreal, as long as it's in the mind of the individual, it's real.

Chief McCormack is also quick to say that if the community thinks it has seen the worst, some major surprises are still in store. The days of the unlocked door are gone forever.

◆ ◆ ◆

Another contributor to crime seems to be our policy on parole and early release of convicts.

At the Sun, I argued that our editorial stance should be that the judge who did the sentencing should get a vote when the parole board wants to give a convict early parole.

I also argued that the paper should support a policy that says that if the suspect who is convicted of a violent crime immigrated to Canada in the last five years, upon conviction, he should be turfed out of Canada.

I spent six years on the police beat for the Tely. The best police story I ever worked on was chronicling the escapades of the notorious Boyd gang.

Eddie Boyd's father was a Toronto policeman and one sister was a missionary. Go figure. The family split up and Eddie left home at fifteen. He grew up to became a small-time crook whose name, initially, meant nothing to most police officers.

In 1948, he robbed a few homes in western Canada, was caught, and did a little time in jail.

By the time he was released, he'd met a few prisoners who convinced him that break-and-entry was small-time stuff. He couldn't wait to try banks.

Shorts

Some of the best reading in a newspaper are short stories usually running the length or width of a page in one column. They need only be one paragraph, just as long as they are interesting.

They occur when an ad or a story are short of what was dummied or, what happens occasionally is, an advertiser instead of buying a full page will purchase four columns which means you wind up with one column of white space across the top and down the side. Logically, what is used to fill this space are called fillers.

Usually editors just fill it with whatever extra is hanging around. That is particularly true of the *Sarasota Herald Tribune* in Florida where we holiday in parts of the winter. When they have extra space they usually fill it with Canadian news. I don't know where they find it but I'll guarantee no paper in Canada is likely to use it.

On the other hand, the Sun works at the problem and fillers have become a well-read part of the paper. Finding extra news is no problem. Every day news gathered from its writers, freelancers, and wire services is about five or six times what is used.

That's why I'm going to try them in some of the following chapters. See if you agree with me.

Here's a sample of what I'm talking about.

Boyd lends an interesting twist to the debate over capital punishment. Throughout his bank-robbing career, he always carried a gun, but there were never any bullets in it.

He and a friend he met in prison held up a bank at the corner of Yonge Street and Lawrence Avenue in Toronto. Someone saw them going into the bank with guns in their hands. Howard Gault, who was Boyd's one-time partner, surrendered on the street outside. Boyd got away from the scene, but a cruiser forced his truck to stop and he was caught without a fight. That was October 16, 1951.

Boyd was linked with five other bank hold-ups. A long sentence awaited him when he got to court. He was being held in Toronto's Don Jail with a couple of very bad guys. William Jackson and Leonard Jackson, who were not related, were forty miles of bad road.

But before police could get them in court, the trio escaped from the Don. It's believed they used a piece of a saw to sever the prison bars. The saw was hidden in Lenny Jackson's wooden foot. They climbed down a forty-foot rope of bed sheets and scrambled over an eighteen-foot wall.

Some thought this acrobatic display was perhaps beyond Lenny Jackson who would have had to accomplish it minus his artificial foot. The deputy governor and two guards were fired and charged.

Boyd said, after he was recaptured, that the three escapers sang "Down by the Old Mill Stream" so the guards wouldn't hear them sawing the bars. If you believe that, you believe in the tooth fairy.

Outside the jail, Steve Suchan, who also had trouble with the law, picked his new-found friends up and drove to a "safe house" in Parkdale.

Safe it wasn't. A jealous former girlfriend of Suchan gave police the license number of his car. This information was given to all police cruisers. The police report called them "armed and dangerous."

Sergeant Eddie Tong was a model detective. He had emigrated from England in 1928 and joined the force in 1929. By March of 1952, three promotions brought him to the rank of sergeant of detectives. Eddie Tong refused an inside job. He knew who was who in the underworld. His partner, Roy Perry, was another dedicated cop.

A few days before, Eddie had told me he'd been to a small city near Pittsburgh to return a prisoner to Toronto. The papers weren't in order and the chief in the city told Eddie he might as well go and come back later. When Eddie returned, there was a new police chief. He met the former one a few minutes later with a dramatically reduced rank. "The wrong guy won the election," he told Eddie.

(Eddie also talked to me about a recent bank hold-up which was not attributed to the Boyd gang. A single robber went into a Leaside bank waving a gun and telling the few customers in the bank not to make a move or he'd shoot.

A deaf customer making a deposit moved and the bandit shot him. The bank manager was so furious he ran to the safe as the bandit left. He got the bank gun — he'd never fired a shot in his life — and ran outside. The bandit was in the back seat, but his driver had stalled the car. The manager took dead aim and pulled the trigger. Just then, the driver got the car going and sped away.

Police looking at the bank's gun later said it had never been fired or serviced. The bullet had literally dropped out of the barrel. The manager had nearly shot himself in the foot.)

Two days after the escape from jail, the Boyd gang were involved in a robbery. They hit a Royal Bank on Roncesvalles Road for $25,000. The next night, at a police raid on a home on Sorauran Avenue, they missed Steve Suchan, who robbed banks with the Boyd gang in between shifts as a doorman at the King Edward Hotel, by half an hour. Both police and criminals knew they were just missing each other. Boyd's decision was to rob another bank.

When Tong and Perry spotted a new Monarch with the license number that had been provided by Suchan's former girlfriend, I have to believe that Eddie Tong knew who was in the car.

It is still a great mystery to me that no back-up was ordered, and after the car pulled to the side of the road, Tong got out and walked almost nonchalantly towards it.

He was within twenty-five feet when shots rang out. Tong pitched face forward, motionless. When they turned him over, his hand was on his gun which was half out of its holster. He had been a second or two too late.

Meanwhile, the gunmen raked the police cruiser. One bullet shattered Perry's arm, but he managed to get to the police radio. "Police officer shot, College near Lansdowne," he gasped.

A couple of us were sitting by the police radio at the Telegram. "That's Roy Perry," I said. "He's with Eddie Tong ... this is it." When the police arrived at the scene, Tong had just enough strength to name his attackers to John Nimmo, chief of detectives.

One day after the shooting, Suchan was shot down in a gun battle in a Montreal apartment. Three bullets hit him, but he lived. Four days later, tough Lenny Jackson was shot four times by police and survived.

Only Boyd remained to be found. Police knew he was hiding, with his wife and his brother Norman, in a Heath Street home.

The good news was that they were going to get Boyd. The bad news was that I was in Hamilton on a phony tip. I did the only thing I could. I called the mayor, Allan Lamport. All the police brass were at his house. As I was speaking to him, Inspector Adolphus Payne was arresting the Boyds without a struggle.

Lampy said he was off to Heath Street in a police cruiser. "Hold them all in the house for one hour and we'll be there," I pleaded with Lampy. He made everyone drink coffee so we could get back from Hamilton in time to take pictures. I'd vote for Lampy if he ran again today, even at his tender age of ninety.

About a week later, Sergeant of Detectives Edward Tong lost his seventeen-day fight for life. A massive blood clot touched his heart and Eddie Tong died immediately, his only company the doctors and nurses who fought so hard to save his life. He had started to slip away the previous day. John Nimmo ignored the "no visitors" warning to get to his friend's side to tell him the Boyd gang was no more. "Good," gasped Tong. It was the last word he spoke.

That should have been the whole story. Shockingly though, in September the four escaped from the Don Jail again. But the Boyd gang were never again to create the excitement they had in the past. The drama was gone. They had no guns, girls or safe houses. They were almost glad to see the police arrive at a deserted farm house in North York a few days later. Their first request was for a meal.

Willie Jackson spent fourteen years in jail and, when last

heard from, was a janitor for a church in Vancouver. Boyd was sentenced to life. He was paroled in 1962. He was put back in jail a few months later for violating parole with a teenage girl. Boyd, if you can believe it, is now a social worker in the west working under an assumed name.

Steve Suchan and Lenny Jackson were hanged back-to-back at the Don Jail.

I spent the entire evening of the hangings sitting with John Robinette and Arthur Maloney. They were satisfied they had done everything they could to avoid the scaffold but every few months, one would go to the phone to see if any intervention had happened. It hadn't and wouldn't.

Suchan and Jackson had two of the best lawyers in Canada but there was little defence they could offer.

At the trial after the two were convicted, Arthur, a leading spokesman against capital punishment in Canada, argued eloquently to avoid the hanging. But it was impossible. Public opinion said no.

In his appeal, he quoted the famous U.S. lawyer Clarence Darrow who, years ago, had spoken eloquently against capital punishment for two young murderers. They avoided the death penalty. Maloney's talk to the jury paralleled Darrow's.

Darrow said: "I have heard in the last six weeks nothing but a cry for blood. I have heard from the office of the State's attorney only ugly hate. They say we come here with a preposterous plea for mercy. When did any plea for mercy become preposterous in this tribunal? If those two boys die on the scaffold, which I can never bring myself to imagine, every newspaper in North America will carry a full report. Every newspaper will be filled with gruesome details. Will it make men better or make men worse? How many will be crueller and colder for it? What influence will it have upon the millions of women who read it? Do I need to argue to the court that cruelty only breeds cruelty? Hatred only causes hatred and all that goes with it — that if there is any way to kill evil and hatred and all that goes through it, it is not through evil, hatred and cruelty. It is often through charity, love and understanding."

An eloquent plea to be sure, and it worked for Darrow. However, I'm sure Maloney knew before he died, that one of those boys killed again in prison.

Anyway, I didn't agree with the anti-hanging lobby. Capital punishment seems just punishment for those who kill police officers and those who commit murder while participating in some other violent crime. The question is, would capital punishment be a deterrent for others? My answer is a resounding yes.

Enough said.

♦ ♦ ♦

While the police desk, crime and stories like the Boyd gang were the stuff of my life then, I knew it couldn't last. I was on my way out as head of the police beat when, in the mid-sixties, I found myself the acting assistant city editor in charge of Saturday and Sunday coverage. I was keen — a little bit over-keen perhaps.

One of the routines I'd initiated on the police beat was visits to the emergency wards of the main local hospitals. We went bearing gifts, mainly chocolates. We also managed to leave a few phone numbers where we could be reached in case something or somebody interesting was brought to the hospital.

This paid off during the second week I was on duty. Sister

Mary Louise at St. Joseph's Hospital called. "Doug, do you know Ace Bailey? He's evidently deeply involved in sports."

"I don't know him personally," I said. "But I know who he is."

Ace Bailey played for the Toronto Maple Leafs and was involved in the most publicized stick fight in the history of the NHL. Bailey had his skull fractured and never played again. But the Leafs kept him as game time-keeper.

"Well," said the Sister, "he was DOA at the hospital this afternoon."

I thanked her for the information and set about arranging real coverage for Monday's paper. We didn't publish Sunday, but the Leafs were playing Saturday evening. I arranged for hockey writer George Gross to write the obituary, stressing the stick fight. Then I got another sports reporter to get tributes to Bailey at the game that night.

Then I thought of my old friend Jack Dennett. His news report on CFRB was the most listened-to newscast in Canada. The Hot Stove Lounge, broadcast from Maple Leaf Gardens between periods on television, also featured Dennett and was also rated number one.

I called him. "Jack," I said. "Ace Bailey is dead." I went on to tell him that no one knew and since we didn't publish Sunday, he could have the exclusive.

Jack wrote his own news and he typed an emotional farewell to Bailey. I heard it on the radio while driving home. I almost cried.

So did Jack when he got to the Gardens to get ready for his television show. The first guy he ran into was Ace Bailey. My Ace Bailey was a bowler.

Ah well, Sister Mary Louise meant well.

Trying To Bid "Adieu" to Monsieur King

To a large extent, it was the characters in this business that made it a happy place to be. Many of them graduated to the police beat but most of them have been eliminated one way or another now. Some have died and some were forced out by non-newspaper people who generally have little interest in the product and thus do not appreciate the vital role these characters play.

George Gross

George Gross was the original sports editor in 1971 of the *Toronto Sun*.

He escaped from his native Czechoslovakia way back when by (a) swimming the Danube River; (b) swimming the Danube River in a hail of bullets; (c) paddling a boat across: (d) paddling a boat across in a hail of bullets or; (e) walking across.

I'm not sure what the real answer is. I've heard him tell it all ways. It seemed to depend on the time of day.

George could speak no English when he arrived in Canada, but he was a quick learner.

He spent some time doing farm work in the Holland

Marsh. Then he went on to Toronto, where he worked for Eaton's in the bargain basement. His main interest, though, was always in sports. He and Steve Stavro, the food supermarket mogul, ran a soccer team in Toronto. The team flopped, but George, characteristically, turned it into a triumph. He had talked his way into the Telegram's sports department as a part-time writer about soccer.

He wound up running the sports department at the Tely and thus was a natural, when it folded, to became the Sun's first sports editor. He was an important and probably indispensable element in our start-up.

But that didn't mean he wasn't a genuine character.

George maintains he quit his job at the Sun more times than anyone else. I maintain he tied with Peter Worthington. George actually has quit one more time than Peter, but George's last resignation came after he had retired and doesn't count.

In our early days, he shimmied up the elevator cable to turn his column in on time. The guy behind him took the elevator.

George loved covering skating, tennis and especially the Olympics and world hockey tournaments. We were pleased with his columns, so George travelled a lot.

Only once was George nearly fired. In San Francisco at one of our Sun directors' seminars, George learned that the *Edmonton Sun* had concluded a great coup by hiring Terry Jones, the number one sports guy in Edmonton, away from the opposition Journal.

I congratulated publisher Elio Agostini, who announced this at our first meeting.

Somehow George believed that Terry had been hired for

more money than he himself was being paid. It wasn't true, of course, but Gross decided to lobby the board of directors anyway.

Former chairman John Grant was the only one who listened to George at any length, and it actually drove John off the wagon.

All that aside, the Baron was and is full value and a good friend. He is as young in mind as men half his age.

Eddie Palmer

Eddie Palmer was a journalist who worked at various times for both the Tely and the major opposition, the *Toronto Daily Star*. For a while he covered City Hall for the Tely. At that time, the councillors sat around an open square. The reporters and photographers had desks in the middle. Eddie got bored easily. He had lost a leg in the war and, when things got too slow for him, he would plunge a newspaper spike into his leg. If that didn't get attention, he would eat (and swallow) a flash bulb or two. I know of at least two councillors who fainted dead away.

When he moved to the Star he lived temporarily in the old Lord Simcoe Hotel. There, every once in a while, he would unscrew his wooden leg and toss it out the window. The police told him he would be jailed if they were called again. Eddie lived on the seventeenth floor of the hotel.

Once, at a party at a colleague's apartment, the landlord climbed the stairs to complain about the noise. Eddie ate his glasses.

Howard Rutsey

Police reporting will never be practised again the way Howard

Rutsey did it. He was straight out of the movie *Front Page*. He looked every inch a senator and that's what we called him.

You could find us most every day, seated in the small police headquarters press room, with radios blaring, and detectives who weren't supposed to be seen with the press whispering confidences. We'd phone houses where trouble was reported, never quite saying whether we were inspectors or not.

It will be said there are many more important things than writing about people in trouble, but it is a necessary part of reporting, and to Howard it was an art.

He was an enthusiast and whatever story he was working on was always the biggest story in the paper to him.

He died from sixty years of living. He was a man who loved a party, a man who had a talent for talking and dancing which could have made him a living in show business, and yet he was devoted to his family and his church.

He was always trying to be a great literary writer and he never was. But he was the finest of reporters, and they are much tougher to find.

Howard Rutsey was a great friend of mine. He was a beggar with million dollar dreams — and he had quite a thirst. One winter evening after we had worked late together on the Tely's police beat, I invited "the Senator" to Marilyn's and my home for dinner. As we reached the Kingsway area, Howard had me stop at a florist shop. He wanted to buy some roses for Marilyn.

He immediately rejected the roses on display, which looked lovely to me. "Selling roses is like renting hotel rooms," he pontificated. "The best ones are always saved for the best customers." The owner dutifully went to the back of his shop and came out with a new bunch of roses.

"They will do," Rutsey said. "Give me two dozen." I think that's the only time in her life Marilyn received two dozen roses.

"How much are they?" the great man asked. "Fifty dollars," said the florist.

"Pay him, will you Doug. I left my wallet at home," Rutsey said.

I used to do that a lot. Not buy roses, but bring guys home at the last minute. Marilyn, God bless her, always seemed ready and produced dinners as if she had all kinds of warning.

That evening we enjoyed one of those good dinners, and then Howard wanted to listen to the big bands with "maybe just one" cognac. Half a bottle later, I decided to go to bed. Howard would listen and drink "one more."

I called Metro Taxi and ordered a cab for Howard at 6:30 a.m.

What happened afterwards, I slept through, but I certainly heard about it.

The alarm awakened Howard at 6:00 a.m. By 6:30 a.m., he had showered and shaved but was in his underwear when he looked out the window to see if it was still snowing — and saw a Metro cab down the street, obviously at the wrong address.

Howard dashed to the phone to call Metro. "Your cab is at the wrong address," he barked.

"Yes, we know, he just called in," the dispatcher replied. "What number are you at?"

Howard had a problem. He didn't know. "Hold on," he said, and went to our front door. Unfortunately, the door faced our driveway and the number was on the front of our house.

Two neighbours walking their dogs had, I guess, seen some queer things at our house but nothing equal to this. A barefoot guy in his underwear shouting through the snow at them: "Where am I?" Then he saw the number and turned back to the house.

Unfortunately, my sister, who lived with us, chose this moment to come up the stairs to be confronted by Howard who tried ineffectually to tell her why he was snow-covered and undressed.

The cab pulled up the driveway. The driver took one look and fled. Howard got dressed and walked to a bus stop.

Possibly we should have saved the roses for another day.

◆ ◆ ◆

If I could choose a career in another life, I'd still want to spend some time on the police beat. The competition was, and still is, fierce.

Jocko Thomas was the *Toronto Star* police beat reporter and Charly Oliver was the Globe's. Howard Rutsey and I were the Tely's. Jocko won two National Newspaper Awards and Charly picked horses on the side for the Globe under the name of Appa Tappas. Both had been around a long time.

It would be fair to say you couldn't get murdered in Toronto without the four of us knowing. It was curiously and splendidly old-fashioned. The city was a more innocent place then; the times less violent and dangerous. Relationships between the press and police were easier. Police headquarters wasn't hostile territory and the police didn't dread the next editions of the papers.

Police reporting certainly hasn't been the same since Rutsey, Charly, Jocko Thomas and I were on the loose in the

Lone Ranger Clayton Moore whose abstinence led to dramatically shortened press conferences.

Toronto — Scarlett Road above Raymore Drive where eighteen houses were destroyed and thirty people died during Hurricane Hazel.

Right: The first *Toronto Sun.* Doug Bassett's presses gave us our start. There have been many Bassetts in our lives. They have been very good to us and for us.

Below: Eclipse building.

Weather
Mainly sunny;
High 60.

Get latest weather changes from
590/CKEY
WEATHER CENTRE

THE
TORONTO SUN

10¢
FINAL

48 PAGES   TORONTO, ONTARIO, NOV. 1, 1971   366-9

Mothballs ...   ... at 1,000 MPI

A $10M GOOF

By BOB MacDONALD
Staff Writer

First night ... 3:00 a.m. ... but Marilyn and I are still smiling!
Photo Credit: Norm Betts

Right: The first *Toronto Sun.* Doug Bassett's presses gave us our start. There have been many Bassetts in our lives. They have been very good to us and for us.

Below: Eclipse building.

First night ... 3:00 a.m. ... but Marilyn and I are still smiling!
Photo Credit: Norm Betts

The Telegram's farewell to Toronto. Parting came hard after ninety-five years.

The Telegram's last day. Bob MacDonald, Don Hunt, George Gross and I finished the champagne and moved on to the Eclipse building.

Above Left: Creighton getting conned in Rome by tailor Angelo Litrico.

Above Right: Howard Rutsey

Left and Below: Boyd gang — upper left-Steve Suchan lower left-William R. Jackson below-Edwin Alonzo Boyd

Lone Ranger Clayton Moore whose abstinence led to dramatically shortened press conferences.

Toronto — Scarlett Road above Raymore Drive where eighteen houses were destroyed and thirty people died during Hurricane Hazel.

Photo Credit: Norm Betts

Myself, Hunt and Worthington relaxing after edition number one. I doubt anyone will do it again.

The Rimstead tour of the Eclipse building.

Photo Credit: Jac Holland

Photo Credit: Norm Betts

Above: Eclipse news room.

Right: For the guy who rarely eats cake, I've sure sliced into a lot in twenty years. This is at the *Edmonton Sun*'s official opening of its new building.

Edmonton staff say good-bye and happy birthday. On day one the presses didn't work — they finally turned over after someone borrowed a car wrench. A few years ago the *Edmonton Sun* gang gave me a replica of the wrench. Reluctantly, I left it in the office as part of our history.

PHOTO COURTESY OF *EDMONTON SUN*

Worthington, MacMillan, Pyette and me. The "A" Team in Calgary on day one.

Photo Credit: Randy Hill

"Fort Hobby" — the *Houston Post*

Three proud publishers reading the first *Financial Post Daily*. From left to right: me, Mr. Neville Nankivelle — who had awaited this day for years — and Frank Barlow of the *Financial Times of London*, the world's best financial paper, in my view.

Photo Credit: Norm Betts

early 60's. I was friendly with some of the younger detectives on the Toronto Police Force and a few of them would sometimes lend me their police identification to help me get past police lines.

The television and radio stations had minimal news staff. Their coverage improved enormously each time a new edition of the Star or Tely hit the streets.

Also, it was well known that the Chief of Police John Chisholm had a clerk detailed to read all the papers and report to him on which of his officers got good reviews.

One day, Rutsey and Chief Chisholm had lunch at Simpson's Arcadian Court. It was a nice summer's day so they walked back to the office.

As they walked down Bay Street, they passed a police constable who paid no attention to them. Chisholm whirled around and went back to him. "Don't you salute your chief?" he shouted. The officer slowly started to salute but clearly had no idea whether Chisholm was chief or was putting him on.

"C'mon John, you're hardly ever downtown, how could you expect this officer to know you?" Rutsey said.

By this time the young officer was saluting at attention. "Stand easy," Rutsey told him. "Now John, you apologize to this young fellow and we'll be on our way." Chisholm, for the first and last time in his career, apologized to a junior officer.

Rutsey took the policeman's name and number and said: "Call me if the chief bothers you." That is certainly one way to maintain good contacts among the regular police officers. If he was anything, Howard was one-of-a-kind, and he did a number of things before anyone else.

He had a great relationship with Toronto Mayor Sam McBride; possibly they became friends because they drank the same brands. And McBride had forgiven Howard for playing a small role in the Tely's campaign in the last election to elect then city editor, Burt Wemp, as mayor.

McBride, the incumbent, had taken to calling Wemp a coward. So the Tely staff got Wemp to bring his military uniform, complete with medals, to work. They helped him onto a kitchen chair and Albert Van, a veteran Tely photographer, lay flat on his back and pictured Wemp standing above him.

The picture looked beautiful on the front page with Wemp seeming seven feet tall. The only caption stated: "This is the man Sam McBride called a coward." Wemp wasn't quite five feet five inches tall.

McBride swept the election.

This meant that the papers had to update the mayor's obituary. Rutsey was assigned the job and spent all day doing it. (Newspapers keep the obituaries of well-known people up-to-date so when they die, a story is ready.)

When he finished, Rutsey ambled up to the members' room at City Hall where politicians and reporters met for a drink at the end of the day. Some also met at the beginning of the day.

There was the mayor teasing: "Where were you Howard; I had an exclusive for you?"

"You couldn't guess," said Howard. "I was rewriting your obituary."

The mayor demanded to see it and after a few libations Rutsey gave in. The mayor read it and started to cry. "You have to get this in the paper, it's the nicest thing I've ever read about myself."

"No way," Howard said, "you have to wait until you're dead." And so he did.

Not long afterwards, Rutsey was assigned to the police beat where I was hanging out. I guess he had celebrated working with me the night before. He had the granddaddy of all hangovers.

I couldn't take much notice because a housewife had been shot to death in Parkdale and I had finally contacted Charlie Cook, the homicide chief, who was on the case.

Howard, meanwhile, had lurched into the seat next to mine and was making a very garbled explanation to his wife of why he hadn't made it home the night before. She hung up on him just as Charlie Cook said: "Okay, here's his name, I'll spell it for you." That's when Rutsey hung up his phone on my cradle. No more Cook and no more story.

Howard also had a broadcast career, although it wasn't nearly as illustrious as his print career. He actually did the first public broadcast of a Queen's Plate horse race in 1932. It was so successful that he was asked back the next year and told he had an extra half hour to describe the colour before the races.

He was at his best. Every prominent person within shouting distance of his booth was dragged in to be interviewed. Howard used up all his glowing adjectives only to find out after his half hour that he misinterpreted a signal and wasn't on the air at all.

All the prominent people got dragged back to be interviewed again.

John McLean
John McLean was a photographer/reporter for the Tely in the 60's. He was once in Ottawa doing a story on the Soviet Embassy when the Canadian government was asked to send

their aircraft carrier, *Homes Magnificent*, to the Gulf as part of a peacemaking effort. British troops had landed in Egypt and the situation was incendiary.

The Canadian media were up in arms because the Navy had ruled it would take no journalists with it.

McLean was one of the hundreds of reporters and columnists trying to get on the ship. The Navy made its first mistake when, responding to the media pressure, they organized a cocktail party on board the night the ship was to sail for the Far East.

McLean was one of the guests. On board, he immediately went to the lifeboats on the far side of the ship, away from the cocktail party.

He loosened the canvas and dumped twenty-four sandwiches his hotel had made up for him and two bottles of rum he'd purchased into a lifeboat. Then he climbed in.

An hour or so later, the *Magnificent* left the harbour and headed for the open sea.

Inside the lifeboat, McLean began his cocktail hour. The sandwiches were uneaten. Hours later, at sunrise in fact, a sailor on guard duty heard someone noisily snoring.

McLean was taken into custody and sent to the commanding officer who correctly concluded McLean was just drunk. But what to do with him?

Then the sailor who had taken McLean into custody, turned up excitedly with McLean's notebook in hand. It contained the names, home addresses, and unlisted phone numbers of seventeen people working in the Russian embassy.

They called the captain. The captain called defense headquarters.

The captain reluctantly turned the aircraft carrier around

and headed back to Halifax. It was later learned, of course, that McLean had obtained the phone numbers of the Russians after throwing a number of caviar and vodka parties in an effort to establish contacts for his Russian embassy story. Twenty-four hours later, the Navy decided their first assessment had been correct — John had simply been drunk.

McLean had another contribution to make for the betterment of journalism.

He was covering the famous Winnipeg flood which, at the time of this escapade, was just finishing up. Things were beginning to calm down, so McLean decided to hold a Miss Winnipeg Flood Worker pageant.

John was the only judge. He declared the winner, and wrote the story with a picture. Then he married the winner.

This is called making the news.

John Chisholm
One Friday morning in July 1958 while I was on a day off, Marilyn and I decided to take our kids to High Park to see the zoo and toss a football around. We parked in the lot next to the restaurant and off we went.

About the same time, police chief John Chisholm telephoned me at the office. When they told him I was on a day off, the chief said he'd call me at home. Also around that time, he telephoned the Star's police reporter, Jocko Thomas. Thomas was out on assignment.

We were both pals of the chief and didn't know that that was the last chance we would have to speak to him. About 9:30 a.m., the chief signed a car out and drove out of the police garage. He'd never been known to drive on his own.

A few minutes later, a traffic officer spotted the chief driving into High Park. He parked in the restaurant lot.

Then he put his gun to his temple and pulled the trigger. Canada's best-known policeman died instantly. No one, to this day, knows why he did it.

It did come out later that one afternoon, a few weeks before he committed suicide, Chisholm had a driver take him to police commissioner Bob Bick's cottage. The driver recalled that the chief from time to time pulled his gun from its holster and examined it. He had never done that before either.

When the car pulled into the Bick driveway, the commissioner, surprised, walked down the driveway to ask the chief in for coffee. Chisholm muttered a greeting to the commissioner, and said he was just in the area and had to get back. He wasn't on the property for more than two minutes.

Speculation was that the chief intended to shoot Bick. Although no one knows for sure, Chisholm did prefer the Toronto chief's job to the larger Metro chief's job which he saw as only giving him more bosses. So Bick got the Metro police commissioner's job with its amalgamation of the areas' six police forces which he had recommended.

Whatever John Chisholm's reasons, it was not reporter Creighton's finest hour. At eleven o'clock that morning the Creighton family was returning home for lunch. We had no knowledge of it, of course, but we walked right past the police car with Chisholm's body in it.

Half an hour later, the phone was ringing. "The chief's body was found by a passer-by. Why the hell didn't you find him?" shouted an editor.

Once again I thought we'd done a better job on the story than the Star, but the only memo I received was a copy of one sent by editorial boss Doug MacFarlane to city editor Art Cole. "Don't let Creighton take a Friday off again," it said.

Jocko and I often wondered if anything would have been different if one of us had been there to answer the phone when Chief Chisholm called.

Monsieur Harold King

His business card said it all for Harold King.

The centre of the card contained his name and underneath it *Chef de Mission* — the *Toronto Telegram* and the *Yorkshire Post*. Beside that was his home address, two office phone numbers, and the following: "After 5:00 p.m. — the Crillon Bar."

The Crillon is one of the three best hotels in Paris. (The Ritz and the George Cinq are the others.) In Harold's view, he was the best reporter in Paris, indeed all of France. Neither the hotel nor King lacked for anything.

Harold was offered his job at the Tely just after he retired as head of Reuters news bureau in Paris. He arranged for John Bassett senior to get an exclusive interview with French president Charles DeGaulle, which paid off with Bassett, who promptly hired him.

Among King's many awards, was the Legion of Honour, France's highest civilian award.

He reported from Stalingrad during the war, both the tragic Russian retreat and, months later, the triumphant forward march which forever broke the German army's morale. This guy was a genuine pro and unfortunately I was coming to Paris with firing him at the top of my agenda. He had a splendid career, of which I knew little.

It had started at budget time. The Tely was losing money, and budget chief Art Holland and I decided it was time to kill the London and Paris bureaus, which would save us about $150,000.

I laid this on publisher Bassett who quickly agreed with London, but seemed somewhat bemused by my plans to close the Paris bureau.

"Let me know how you make out with Harold King," he said as I left. "I'll be very interested."

Marilyn came along with me. London was easy. I think Ron Poulton wanted to go home soon anyway. He already knew he was slated to become chief of the CFTO-TV news department. Bassett owned the television station as well as the newspaper.

Paris was a different story. Before we had even cleared customs in France, an immaculately dressed fellow wearing a chauffeur's cap identified himself to us and said his car was parked in front for us.

"How did you know us?" I asked.

"I studied the picture that Mr. King gave me," he replied.

Customs was a breeze. We were waved through with only a perfunctory stamping of passports. Our bags had disappeared into the trunk of the car which certainly was parked out front, precisely between the "no parking" signs. It was a large Citroën.

We were taken to the Crillon Hotel where our bags disappeared again, winding up unpacked in our suite before we got there.

Harold King emerged from the bar to welcome us to France just as the front desk told us we had already been checked in — by Mr. King, of course.

"Come with me," he said. "We'll have a little respite before you clean up for lunch." There at a corner table, guarded by three waiters, was our "little respite" of caviar and smoked salmon. Nor were we to go thirsty, with a choice of champagne, vodka or chablis.

"Please use my Citroën and driver while you're here," Harold said between bites.

Somehow, during our respite, I didn't get around to firing Harold. Instead, we marched to our rooms to clean up for the next meal.

I told Marilyn to stay in the room or go shopping. My meeting might be difficult.

At lunch, new liquor and wine bottles had replaced the slightly used ones. The menu was a complete evening's read.

I decided to take the direct approach. "Harold," I said. "I had better tell you right now that I'm here to wind down the Paris bureau." Harold looked bemused.

"Did you speak to John about this?" he asked.

"Yes, I did," I replied, "but I must say his reaction to Paris was not the same as it was to London."

"I report directly to John," Harold said coolly. "As a matter of fact, I'm staying with him and Isabel (Bassett's wife) next month. "I'll tell you what I'll do. I'll tell him to put me on his budget."

It dawned on me that I had been blind-sided by my friendly publisher. As I reflected on this, Harold announced abruptly that he'd forgotten an interview he had to do in half an hour. He hoped I wouldn't mind lunching alone. And, oh yes, the interview would likely last well into the evening so we wouldn't be going to the Crazy Horse Saloon that night.

He left quickly, never to resurface on that trip. Nor did we see the Citroën or driver again. I was surprised Harold didn't have the hotel downgrade our suite.

Back in Toronto, Bassett praised me for closing the

London bureau. "We have to tighten up," he said. "How did you make out in Paris?"

"King told me he'd tell you personally when you meet him on the Riviera next week," I said.

Fortunately, we did meet Harold King again. We visited the Bassetts at their villa near Nice, where we witnessed a battle between him and Bassett over who would order lunch for the group meeting at a four-star restaurant in the mountain town of Èze.

Bassett won and ordered barbecued chicken for the bunch of us. There was no argument about who would pay the bill. Harold was beaten without a vote.

He was so furious about "eating Colonel Sanders" in a world class restaurant that he made Marilyn and me stay and he ordered another meal for us. I never told him, but I preferred the chicken.

We saw him again several times when he visited Toronto. He even wrote a few pieces for the Sun. He died in 1991 — one of journalism's giants.

Doug MacFarlane

Doug MacFarlane, sometimes affectionately called "Bigdome," was likely the best editor I ever worked for. He had been hired from the Globe by the Telegram to supervise the newsroom and improve the editorial content of the Tely. He did that in spades.

And he did it with flair and a sense of drama.

Almost all of us remember where we were when President John F. Kennedy was shot and killed. I was in the Cork Room bar across the street from the paper having lunch with Marilyn when the owner came downstairs and plugged in a television set so the patrons could watch the coverage. I left

Marilyn there and rushed back to the office with Charlie Nicol, the news editor.

This was the kind of developing story that tested newspapers most. Radio and television can handle new developments by simply reading them on the air. Newspapers must edit the information, get it in type on a page, get it all to a press and then into the delivery process. Meanwhile the story keeps developing. (The Sun, at its best, could do it in seven minutes.)

The first wire service reports had little other than the shooting of the president. Soon, though, came reports of the wild ride to the hospital and the brief, breathless wait for JFK to die. Soon we had reports of a police officer shot in a theatre and then the arrest of Oswald.

MacFarlane had taken over the Tely's city desk from the city editor and was doing what he was very good at. He had just approved the final proof of our home delivery edition when the bulletin about Oswald's arrest arrived.

MacFarlane turned and pointed dramatically at Jerry Pratt, who was in his fourth week of a trial to become an assistant city editor.

"Pratt, go down and stop the presses," said MacFarlane.

"How do I do that?" Pratt asked politely.

"Put your goddamned fingers in it if you have to," replied MacFarlane.

A few years later at the Sun, MacFarlane played an innocent cameo role in a drama starring Peter Worthington, who was editor of the Sun and carried that title. Peter had been editor, and a most effective one, since day one. We'd clashed and he quit the odd time, but secretly I'm sure that despite our differences, we've been like-minded most of the time.

Eddie Monteith had run the Sun newsroom day and night for almost five years. He wanted to settle into a late afternoon/ evening shift until he retired and we wanted him to do it. Certainly, he deserved whatever he wanted. He typified what was best about the Sun.

That left a leadership role vacant day-to-day in the newsroom. Inside the Sun organization, Hartley Steward was by yards the best candidate. But I had been having a few exploratory chats with MacFarlane who, after he left the Telegram, had worked for and retired again from Royal LePage. He was presently playing out the string running the Ryerson School of Journalism. I thought if I could get two years out of JDM, as he was also known, we would professionalize the newsroom.

This decision devastated Hartley, also one of my best friends. He ignored the argument that two years was not long to wait. He liked JDM but thought any suggestion he couldn't do the job as well as JDM was nonsense. He quit and went to the Star. He was right and I was wrong. He made managing editor at the Star. He phoned to have dinner and made me eat crow, then said he wanted to come back to the Sun.

I had consulted Worthington about my plans to hire JDM. His memory has blurred on this, but initially he agreed with it. Then we started to play the title game. We wound up agreeing to call MacFarlane editorial director, appearing in a different spot on the masthead so as not to appear to conflict with Peter's editorial role. But it was a problem for Peter.

His first move was to whistle down to the composing room. He got Peter Simpson, the editorial page compositor, and had him change his title to editor-in-chief. Not being a regular reader of mastheads, I didn't notice, but MacFarlane did and called me.

"What are you going to do about it?" he asked. After due reflection I took what was viewed as an unusual route albeit effective.

"Congratulations on your appointment," I wrote Peter. "You deserve it. You have been indispensable to the Sun." I received no reply.

About three weeks later, I got a call from Peter from the first class Air Canada lounge. This must be serious, I thought, because he tells me he always flies economy and he wouldn't want me to know he was flying first class. He played the same sort of game with us over company cars. Peter always pointed out that he had a smaller car than either Don Hunt or I. I checked one day and he was right. It was smaller but he had ordered every extra known to man on it.

I must confess to the directors that if Peter had wanted a Jaguar, he could have had it from me. He is a great tabloid journalist, although a flaming shit disturber.

Worthington was furious when he reached me from the first class lounge. I had demoted him, he claimed. That day's paper had him back to editor.

I guess I should have taken it seriously, but having had nothing to do with it, nor any knowledge of it, I broke into loud laughter. Peter hung up. But not before he quit — again.

It finally unfolded that Peter Simpson, Worthington's original unwitting co-conspirator, was to blame. He'd dropped the editorial page on the floor and stepped on the masthead, dirtying it. He replaced it with an old one, which had Peter as editor, also by mistake.

I decided I wouldn't perpetuate things with a clever note about Peter taking a step back. I thought I'd leave well enough alone and I never heard anything more about it.

CHAPTER 5

The Old Lady of Melinda Street

The Bassetts, John and Johnny, father and son, have played an important part in my life and in the life of my family. They have had a powerful influence on my life as a journalist, which is how I would like to be remembered: as a journalist, not as a businessman, where some of my experiences have left only scars.

I remember telling a writer from *Toronto Life* magazine in 1971, who was pursuing a story on the Tely closing, that whatever the world might think of Big John, he was my kind of person.

I think the same today and I'd add Bassett Junior.

Those of us privileged enough to have been friends of Johnny Bassett remember the special moments with him during his lifetime. He died at age forty-seven in 1986. He left us with so much yet before him. Nonetheless he had accomplished more, in so many fields, than one would think possible for one man.

Johnny marched to his own drummer and was a man of causes. He practically founded a new professional hockey league and a new professional football league. He promoted world class car racing in Ontario. A Davis Cup tennis player, he later relived those glories through his talented daughter Carling.

He was an innovative and creative entrepreneur. He produced the rock musical, *Hair*, in Canada. He created and produced television shows at CFTO and a teenage special section called "After 4" at the Telegram newspaper. But above all, he constantly thought of his family.

So many of us live in the afterglow of Johnny's life, exemplified best, I think, by his friend and Sun director, Rudy Bratty, who said: "Johnny and I were born on opposite sides of the railroad tracks, but when I was with him, he made the tracks disappear." Johnny was born to privilege, yet had such a common, comfortable touch with everyone.

In his final months Johnny's cause was the Rudy Falk Oncology Centre. Dr. Falk gave Johnny hope. John returned the favour by encouraging him to open his clinic in 1985.

John Bassett Senior was the first Bassett I met. I was a young reporter at the Telegram. It was winter and he was wearing a wonderful fur coat. He looked more like a movie star than a publisher.

The day before, I'd received a brief personal memo from him congratulating me for winning an award from the Fire Fighters Association for a story on a fire and fire fighting. That evening, a mutual friend told me that John Bassett had told him that I had "a very promising career ahead of me."

So I looked forward to meeting him as we both walked towards the elevator.

"How are you, Bob?" he asked, flashing that great smile of his as he shouldered me aside. I was crushed, literally and figuratively. The next day we met again at the elevator. The

Telegram was unionized and I had voted for it and helped minimally in the organization of it. I'd started cooling towards it when Roly, the elevator operator, insisted on calling all his passengers "brother."

Like practically everyone at the Tely, Roly liked his beer. Most days he'd have just one more pint at lunch which would leave him no time to eat. Back at work, he'd park between floors and eat a sandwich on the elevator. He was holding a ham and tomato sandwich when the elevator door opened to reveal Bassett and me waiting to get on.

Knowing he was in trouble with the publisher, he tried desperately to shove the sandwich into his inside coat pocket. It missed and as I was trying to explain to John Bassett that my name was Doug, not Bob, a piece of Roly's sandwich hit the floor. We all had a good laugh. John Bassett never called me Bob again.

For several weeks after the Tely unionized I took the stairs and avoided the elevator. Roly could call someone else "brother."

It should be said here unequivocally that among Johnny's many great ideas was the formation of a morning tabloid paper. In late 1966, Johnny Bassett and I failed to impress his father with a pitch to start a morning tabloid paper to compete against the Globe, as well as publishing the Telegram against the Star in the afternoon. Big John said he didn't like tabs and that was that. In the early days of selling advertising for the Sun, though, we used the dummy pages that Johnny and I had prepared in 1966.

A year or so later, while I had no figures, I sensed that the Tely had started to lose money. Johnny and I made another visit to his dad. We got the same response to a somewhat different argument.

This time we wanted to turn the Tely into a morning tab leaving the Star by itself in the afternoon. People in Toronto don't like tabs, John claimed. And he added ominously that he was beginning to doubt that there was room for three daily newspapers in Toronto — let alone four.

So a few months later I listened very carefully to Jack Callen, a vice-president of Air Canada, who offered me a job as a public relations man for the airline in Toronto and points west.

It was for substantially more money than I was making and I nearly took it. But at the last moment, the printers' ink in my blood overcame good sense and I told Jack I was staying in the newspaper business. Marilyn and I later became very good friends of Jack and his wife, Bernice.

In the early summer of 1971, Marilyn, our son Bruce, and I took off for London for a brief theatre tour. We were with Johnny Bassett, his wife Susan, and their daughter Vicky.

That first night in London, we found a sitter for the kids and went to the theatre. The girls were tired afterwards and went back to the Inn on the Park. Johnny and I decided we'd have one for the ditch.

After the third ale, I swore John to secrecy and told him I'd turned down a job at Air Canada. He didn't say much and I dropped the subject.

A few days after I returned to work at the Tely. The publisher arrived around 10:00 a.m., which was very early for him.

"Let's break a rule and have a martini for lunch," he said. At noon we were seated in the Franz Josef Room of the old Walker House, my favourite eating place at the time.

John Senior wasted no time. "I understand you turned

down a good job with Air Canada," he said.

"Your son is a big loudmouth," I said. "He promised not to tell you."

"You'll thank him after you hear what I have to say," John said. "But right now, finish your drink and go and phone that guy and ask him if it's too late to change your mind."

"That's a damned lousy way to get rid of your managing editor," I sputtered.

"I'm going to close or sell the newspaper," he said.

I was stunned. He told me the Telegram was losing more than one million dollars a year and he had initiated talks with the Star. "Geez, can't you sell it to anyone but them?" I said. "They're the enemy."

To tell the truth, I can't remember anything more about the lunch, but I did organize some time with Jack Callen who kindly said it wasn't too late to change my mind.

Nothing had leaked out by early September, but Bassett told me negotiations were reaching a critical stage.

While he didn't say it, I knew the publisher was desperately trying to find some reason to change his mind. His only hope appeared to be a final meeting of the union members. He felt sure "his boys" would vote for the company's offer of a two-year contract with an across-the-board raise of ten dollars in each year.

The union executives knew Bassett couldn't afford even that. He let them have their own auditor examine the books. He thought they would take it. Surprisingly, a large majority voted to strike. If the vote had been different, I feel sure he would have found a way to hang in, at least temporarily. I don't know, however, if the Telegram could have been saved in the long run. We'd likely gone too far.

Anyway, we were down the tubes, as they say. The only thing left to do was to announce it.

Mrs. Kmiciewicz, known universally as Mrs. K., ran the Tely switchboard. It took me a few years to realize just how good she was. She was feisty and had a sharp tongue when the occasion warranted it. That final union meeting became very acrimonious, and most of us knew the vote to strike had sealed the fate of the Telegram.

One of the more obnoxious reporters had told the meeting that he would rather shovel snow for a living than accept John Bassett's niggardly offer.

The next morning Mrs. K. marched over to his desk and handed him two dollars. "That's a deposit on your snow shovel," she said. "I hope you use it."

Mrs. K. later joined the Sun, and exemplified much of what we stood for.

I finally felt obligated to break my promise of silence to Bassett because Eddie Monteith, the Tely's news editor, and one of the best, told me he had turned down a similar job with the *Kitchener-Waterloo Record* for more money.

I asked him for dinner and told him what was happening. Ironically, when I returned home, there was a note from my son Donald. "Big Bassett called, he's at the office."

Bassett was in his office typing his farewell message to the staff. With him, besides myself, was the company lawyer, Charles Dubin (now Chief Justice of Ontario) and Don Poitras, his labour negotiator (now deceased).

We were all there to help, but he wouldn't accept it.

"It's my responsibility," he said, as he ended a brief message which announced he would close the paper on October 30th. "I'm sorry I couldn't do better," he wrote.

The Telegram was called the "Old Lady of Melinda Street." It had lasted for eighty-seven years. I was there for twenty-three of them. Parting comes hard no matter what the cause. But when you knew the old girl had been kicked to death by a combination of inept union negotiators and bad management, as I did, there was blind anger along with the grief. Whenever a good newspaper dies, everyone loses. When a great paper like the Tely was in its heyday expires, the loss is immeasurable.

When I first started at the paper, under the team of McCullagh and Bassett, you could feel the excitement of change. Up until that time, the "Old Lady" was grey and going nowhere. About the most exciting thing in the place had been Ray Snider, the shipping writer. Snider wore a bowler hat every day he came to work and he kept it on until he reached home after shift.

Every Armistice Day, the Telegram hired a trumpeter to play the Last Post. He would stand behind Ray's desk with the window open so the people passing by on Bay Street could hear. Invariably, they stopped for a minute of silence. But the big news was in the fourth floor editorial department where Ray took off his bowler for the only time in the year. And yes, he had hair.

The new dynamic duo of McCullagh and Bassett were determined to bring youth into the paper. As mentioned, they hired five of us from *Canadian High News*, including Stan Houston and me. The paper unquestionably improved. Competition between the Star and the Telegram was as fierce as in any city anywhere — and it was great fun.

The Star had deeper pockets, mainly because they carried the overwhelming majority of classified advertising. They outstaffed the Tely on every major story.

It became quite clear that over the years, slowly but surely, the Telegram was slipping financially. In 1965, when compositors at all three papers threatened a strike, the Tely had
the most to lose.

That year, Marilyn and I and the kids were training it
across the country and had reached Vancouver when the
compositors went on strike. The Tely at least was prepared.
In fact, for several days we were able to bail out the Star or
Globe by making up some of their pages for them.

Big John gave one of his best speeches ever during that
time, standing on the circulation dock. He told the assembled
staff that the paper would remain in the Bassett family and, as
one of the boys, pleaded with the other unions to ignore the
compositors' strike. They did. It was one of his finest hours.
The three papers never missed a day printing and gradually
the picketers disappeared.

The union had one card left and, to my surprise, it worked.
Correctly thinking the Telegram was the weakest of the three
papers, they visited the Tely's home delivery readers and
advertisers, asking them to boycott the newspaper.
Thousands did. It was the last kick at the can by the union,
but the Old Lady took a huge financial hit.

A couple of years before, the composing staff had walked
out, having mistakenly thought they could shut down at least
one of the Toronto papers. They never got back inside, and
the other paper unions honoured their contracts and stayed in.

During the 1965 strike, I was driving out of the Tely parking
lot with Annis Stukus, a former all-star football player and
then a Tely sports columnist. Stukus was a big man and when
a few picketers stopped my car, Stukus got out ominously.

"Whose work are you doing, sir?" yelled one guy. "I'm doing yours and yours and yours," Stukus said, pointing at three different picketers. The picket line opened up.

Meanwhile Bassett Senior was working a different street. He and a group of Conservative caucus members and big business Tories decided John Diefenbaker had outlived his usefulness as prime minister.

They launched an assault on him which didn't work even though Big John himself had written the editorial supporting Lester Pearson, the Liberal leader.

It read in part:

"Rarely have Canadians been so confused and uncertain about their political choices. The election campaign has not clarified this confusion for the voters. Canadians must make their choice thoughtfully and seriously — the Telegram has done so.

The newspaper believes the best interests of Canada can now be served by the election of Mr. Pearson and his Liberal party."

Since Bassett never did anything in halves, most of Canada thought he was leading the charge against Diefenbaker, and some of them were damned mad. Some knew how they would pay him back. They would stop reading his paper. Almost 10,000 did and a lot of them never returned. It was another blow to the "Old Lady."

During the 1965 strike I was sports editor. I missed the first day of the strike flying home from Vancouver. Our sports composing room was run by a pickle farmer from

Bradford named Harry. John Webb was the number two compositor on the pages. We found out after a couple of weeks that he was a union plant. Webb decided he liked us and played true confessions with management. He quit the union and soon after was made head of the composing room.

After several months, Webb convinced himself he was easily the best man in all of production and attacked the existing management. He lost, quit and went to work for General Motors. It was there that I found him when we were going to start our own composing room at the Sun.

Webby is volatile, a back-stabber on occasion, egotistical and the best production man I've ever met. We needed him. We had found out quickly that none of us knew anything about production, so Webby instantly became part of the inner circle.

I am not fond of many meetings, nor of long meetings. I think they create a vacuum in search of leadership and a potential forum for dissent. Webby agreed, so we set up a one-on-one relationship in which we rarely trusted each other.

He started hiring staff. I heard the first condition of employment in Webb's empire was that the applicant, if he was a union member, had to tear up his membership card in front of Webb. It occurred to me this was likely breaking some law, so I just pretended I didn't hear it.

During the four weeks between the announcement of the closure of the Tely to the launch of our new paper, I spent nearly as much time with Bassett and his wife, Isabel, as I did with future investors and worrying about the content of the Sun.

That brought me into the Franz Josef Room once more, this time at my expense. My guest was Big John who listened to my newest plea in silence.

I explained the Sun would not offer home delivery; therefore, it was paramount that we own the Tely's 2,200 newspaper vending boxes. Further, I told him, we could not be a responsible paper without a library — the Tely library. Finally, I simply asked for the Telegram syndicate, which sold material to other papers and was making about $50,000 annually.

I mentally pictured what was going on in Big John's mind. He had closed a paper, his most prized possession. "You can put being president of a television station in your hat compared to being publisher of a paper like the Telegram," he often told me.

And he really wasn't at all sure the Sun could make it. Nonetheless he proved to be one of our biggest cheerleaders, and is to this day.

"Douglas," he boomed. "Let me tell you what I've done about those things. I've sold the boxes to the *Globe and Mail*, I've sold the syndicate to the Star, and I've given the library to York University.

"But get me Joe Garwood on the phone and I'll reverse everything." He did. Later he admitted he told the president of York he wasn't getting the library — "for now. When the Sun goes belly-up, Creighton promises to give it back to you."

I wasn't planning anything of the kind. That lunch was the most important one I had at that time. Some of the others gave us the money. This gave us the tools to do the job.

Now we were all going in a more promising direction —
forward. And we were doing it the best way to do it —
together. Well, almost.

I rushed back to the office to tell the key players that the
dream of most newsmen to start their own paper was full
speed ahead. I couldn't reach Don Hunt. He was at the
Osgoode Hall court buildings where he was suing John
Bassett for a year's severance pay.

CHAPTER 6

The Sporting Life

A s the last days of the Telegram faded away, Hunt, Worthington and I were making necessary decisions without any real background on which to call.

Every editorial person I've ever talked to says how great it would be to have journalists running their papers. I agree, but we really did need the three of us.

Don Hunt was putting together our circulation department. Don was a journalism graduate from the University of Western Ontario. He had had some background in public relations, helping Johnny Bassett in a failed attempt to bring a major car race to Toronto. When that went sour, Johnny brought him back to the Telegram where he ran the Tely syndicate until the paper finally expired.

Peter Worthington was a reporter, a great reporter, likely the best I've ever worked with. I don't think he wanted to be in management, preferring to be where the action was. As it turned out, he was perfectly suited to run his editorial pages and the columnists he hired to write for them. Throughout his tenure as editor, the pages were always the second or third best-read in the paper. That was almost the opposite of readership figures at most other papers, where the editorial and op-ed pages usually trail far behind sports and entertainment. Page one, of course, is always number one.

Peter, I think, loved that job. He also loved office intrigue and contributed to it — or started it — regularly. He was a world class shit disturber. Although I was occasionally the victim, I say it enviously. He and switchboard boss Mrs. K. could turn the whole place upside down in a couple of hours.

One thing Peter was not was an executive. He joined Hunt and me from time to time, and contributed his ideas occasionally, but he wanted no part of making daily decisions in other departments.

Then there was me. My only newspaper experience was in editorial. That was extensive, since I'd been a general reporter, police and court reporter, assistant city editor, sports editor, city editor and managing editor at the Tely.

As managing editor of the Telegram, I learned that the Tely didn't have an editorial budget. Art Holland (who was on the city desk at the time) and I did one from scratch. The total was just slightly less than it took us to run the Sun for the first year.

I guess because I had spent time with Johnny Bassett trying to sell his father on the idea of starting a tabloid, my partners decided I should be publisher. I preferred to think it was my good looks and personality. Actually, I knew I had the job but I can't remember we three ever talking about it. Later on, however, I think Don might have voted otherwise.

I did wonder and worry about what the investors might be thinking. I tried to practice a knowing look which I could use on them. If there was a tough question, I gave them the look and said wisely, if untruthfully on occasion: "Yes, of course

I know that. However, I haven't looked at it recently. I'll take a look and get back to you."

It seemed to work, although the only thing the bankers wanted was to install their own financial guy. We said absolutely not. If he works for us, he reports to us. They finally agreed.

I simply took the stance then, and subscribe to it now, that success is not forever, and failure is not necessarily fatal. The courage to keep struggling is what counts. So I just kept on making decisions.

I suspect that my previous experience as sports editor gave me the most business experience because most of the people I dealt with there were successful business people.

The sporting life I inherited as Tely sports editor in 1965 and 1966 was likely the most enjoyable two years of my life. My first discovery was the Sport of Kings — horse racing.

Of necessity, there's a lot of wealth in racing. It has its rogues, of course, and more than its share of characters, even among the powerful businessmen who wouldn't talk to you from behind their office desks, but were on a first-name basis with you at the track.

Now, unfortunately, the recession has gotten even the Jockey Club in difficulty, with crowds and betting down substantially. Even the waiters who used to run your bets to the mutuel windows are gone — victims of the economy.

But in the good old days, E.P. Taylor was a wildly successful developer and the man mainly responsible for the existence of Woodbine race track — one of the world's best, in my view. E.P. never even returned my calls when I was a reporter.

When I became sports editor, though, it was a different story. I'd had the sports editor's job for about six months when one day my phone rang. "Doug, it's Eddie. Have you got a minute?"

"I'm sorry, do I know you?" I ventured.

"It's Eddie Taylor from the Jockey Club," he said. "Have you got a lunch time available? I want you to come over to 10 Toronto Street for a meal. I want your advice on something. It'll be just the two of us."

"How about noon today?" I replied, trying to sound cool.

It was 11:30 a.m. then. Time has taken away my memory of what we talked about. But I do remember that "Eddie and Doug" had a great lunch.

A few months later, I was promoted to city editor, and a month or so after that I phoned my friend Eddie to see if we could have lunch. He wasn't available. His secretary took my number, but he never called back.

A couple of years before the Tely crisis, Ray Timson, the retired managing editor of the Star, and I were attending the same journalism course in New York at a hotel owned by Columbia University.

One day we received an "urgent" phone message to call Don McGregor at his brokerage office in Toronto. Don used to buy trotters in Australia and break them in at small Ontario tracks. If he thought the horse was a good one, he'd send it to Roosevelt Raceway outside New York.

Don had a trotter called Auchincraig at the track running in the sixth race that night, but he couldn't leave Toronto.

"Do you have $1,000?" he asked. There was no way we did so we took off from our class and went to Wall Street and picked up the $1,000 from a friend of Don's.

Ray and I placed Don's bet of $1,000 to win.

Well into the excitement of the evening, we invested most

of our own dough, including coupling Don's horse with everything else in the race in the exacter. (To win an exacter, the two horses you bet on must finish first and second.)

Auchincraig ran away from the field. He won by six lengths and paid twenty-eight dollars for every two dollars invested. McGregor was $14,000 ahead, helped along by a $500 exacter and other assorted bets. Timson and I won about $3,000 between us and brought our wives down to New York for a great weekend.

Convinced I'd found an easy way to make money without working, I called a travel agency friend, the late Gordon Alexander, and suggested we buy a horse for ourselves. Gordon and his wife, Mickey, went to the trotting races as often as they could. Both of us had trouble getting away in the afternoon for the thoroughbreds, so Gordon suggested we buy a trotter because they raced in the evening.

We hired a trainer, borrowed $35,000 between us, and waited to buy our first horse. Marilyn and I were golfing in California when we got the call from Gordon. We had bought a horse at an auction for $18,000. Her name was Tic Tac Tina. This called for an immediate meeting to discuss the colours for our one-horse stable.

Interspersed in these serious deliberations was the odd toast to Tic Tac Tina. We all went to bed happy, but the phone rang at 6:00 a.m. It was Gordon. "Tic Tac Tina is dead," he said. "She was electrocuted in a horse walker."

Filled with sorrow, I asked: "Who owned her?" Gordon was able to tell us the ownership had not been transferred, so we still had our money.

Next time our trainer went to Ottawa for a horse sale. We used up only $16,000 for a grey trotter called, aptly, Sun Ray

Precious. The trainer shipped him to Toronto and on to Mohawk Raceway for his debut under new owners.

As the two couples walked into the track, we heard that our horse was a late scratch by the track veterinarians. The trainer said he developed pneumonia. I said: "No doubt he got it at Tic Tac Tina's funeral."

Gordon, the wizard, negotiated a way to send him back to Ottawa, and we did.

Next came Jeff Surge. He had to qualify when he finished first in a no betting race. A few days later, he was at Greenwood Raceway in Toronto for his inaugural. So were we, his proud new owners. Our horse was ahead at the final turn. He was battling it out with two other horses when Jeff broke stride and started to pace. He finished eighth and we finished with him. We got a few bucks back when he was used on the farm as a stud.

We retired officially as owners.

My favourite quote from the race track came from Jack Stafford. He made his money mainly from jam, but he got a lot back from the horses.

He gave a lot also. When the Tely folded, Jack was among the first on the phone. He had two farms for his thoroughbreds in Port Elgin on Lake Huron. He also owned the weekly *Port Elgin Times*, which was about to close.

"I'll sell it to you," he said. "Pay me when you can." We actually did look at it, but besides being editor, one would also have had to run a small china department as well as a card department.

I thought I'd leave the tea cosies to someone else.

Jack won the Queen's Plate twice in a row. The first year, the Queen gave him the traditional fifty guineas. The second year, the Queen Mother handed over the gold. "Say, Your Highness," Jack said to her. "I met your daughter last year. She's a great girl. Give her my best when you get back to London."

I met the Queen Mother at a brunch in 1992. She remembered the incident immediately.

◆ ◆ ◆

The World Series Champion Blue Jays are selling out and are again threatening to go all the way. Having said that, I think hockey is still number one in the fans' hearts.

When the Toronto Maple Leafs made the playoffs last year (1993) and eliminated the favourite Detroit Red Wings, Marilyn and I started to use our tickets again. As was normal several years ago, we returned to George Bigliardi's Steak House on Church Street. George is noted for his food, and this year every playoff game was like a reunion for all of us who had been giving tickets away. Now we were back on the scene. George's cash flow jumped dramatically.

My relationship with the Leafs started simply enough. Sun sports editor George Gross and I met Leaf coach Punch Imlach in the Franz Josef Room for lunch. The regular hockey season was over and, for a change in the Imlach era, the Leafs had missed the playoffs.

Gross' idea was to sign up Punch to help cover the playoffs for us. Punch was eager and we had the deal wrapped up before we started lunch. Of course, it called for a champagne toast.

We started for the door about 2:00 p.m., but we didn't get far. Punch spotted an adjoining bar — The Swiss Bear — and suggested one cold beer couldn't hurt us. While sipping, I spotted Hamilton Tiger Cat Bernie Faloney sitting alone at the bar. I said I'd ask him to join us.

"That is not Bernie Faloney," Imlach said. "I can't stand guys like you coming into sports and a month later becoming world class experts. He had a point, but I had met Faloney and had also interviewed him. I went to the bar. He remembered me and we walked back to the table.

"Bernie Faloney," I said, "meet Punch Imlach."

"Bernie and I are friends," Imlach lied, "I tried to tell him that was you at the bar but he said it wasn't." That put Punch safely on both sides of the argument. I retreated but got even later on.

Punch remembered he had two assignments that evening. He had promised Leaf owner Harold Ballard he'd look at a good prospect playing that night at Maple Leaf Gardens, and after that he'd promised to take his wife Dodo to dinner. It was not to be. George and I escorted him to Maple Leaf Gardens and ran into Ballard, who invited us for another drink, as if we needed it.

After a few minutes, Punch remembered Dodo was meeting him at the Gardens. "Why don't you sit up in the greens," I suggested, "she'd never think to look there."

"Great idea," said Punch and, much the worse for wear, walked out. A few minutes later, Gross and I went to the arena to catch a bit of the game.

I glanced up at the green seats and saw one person. There, surrounded by hundreds of empty seats, was Punch, sound asleep.

Before we could mount an escape plan, Dodo had joined him. Overall, Punch won more than he lost in his career at the Gardens. Not this time.

Punch and Dodo left, but George and I joined Ballard after the game. At one stage, John Robertson, a fine sports writer and a true character, locked us temporarily in the steam room.

Harold drove me home. I have no idea why he would drive in his condition and why I would let him. But we arrived safely. My wife met me inside the front door. "What have you been doing?" she snarled.

"Don't worry," I said, "I've been out with Howard Billard."

Marilyn called him that from time to time until he died. As for Harold, he sent her flowers every Christmas.

I am, of course, aware of the bad reputation Harold carried to his grave. However, he was always helpful and nice to me. When I became sports editor I took a few trips with the Leafs. In those days, the Leafs played every Saturday night and often were back-to-back with the same opponent on Sunday.

Most of those weekends, I'd get a call from Ballard to join him. Then Ballard, Dave Keon, King Clancy and I would go walking. Clancy and Keon would find a Catholic church. Ballard and I would continue walking, then we'd all meet for a Bloody Mary.

Once I fronted for a group led by Peter Widdrington of Labatt's, who wanted to buy the Gardens. As I recall, the stock was selling for around thirty-seven dollars. The group offered fifty dollars, but my partners would have let me go to sixty dollars. Harold thought it over for about ten seconds and said "no." One of the reasons, he said, was that he was sure the stock would hit one hundred dollars.

"Harold," I said, "there is no way the stock will go that far.

If your stock hits one hundred dollars, I'll kiss your butt on the City Hall steps." A few months later, Harold called me to say he was waiting for me on the City Hall steps. I looked up the Gardens share price in the Sun. It had hit one hundred dollars. Harold let me out of my bet.

Together with *Toronto Star* sports editor Milt Dunnell and sports columnists Jim Coleman and Red Foster, I gave character evidence for Harold when he was charged with spending shareholders' money on himself. The judge — a great racing and hockey fan — asked us many questions, making the appearance a lot of fun. When it was all over, though, he sent Harold to Kingston Penitentiary for three years.

While Harold was on his way to Kingston in a police van, John Robinette, his lawyer, was hosting a luncheon at Winston's for us four character witnesses.

Robinette said Ballard had not wanted to ask us to give evidence, but he had been talked into it by Robinette, who said our testimony would make the difference between a sentence of two years less a day which would be served in a reformatory, as opposed to two years, which would be served in a penitentiary.

"Since he received three years," Robinette said, "I can only thank you and predict no one else will use you as character witnesses." He was right.

Ironically, Harold didn't need to go to jail. Known as a good friend of Harold's, I was approached to tell him that the charges against him would be dropped, or at the very worst, a guilty plea would result in a suspended sentence, if he would testify at Stafford Smythe's trial. Stafford, another Gardens owner, faced similar charges.

Ballard declined. "He's a friend of mine." Smythe died

before his trial could be held.

Marilyn and I visited Harold in the penitentiary a couple of times. It looked like he had everything under control. The guards saluted us as we drove in the front gates. Marilyn had bags full of his favourite peanut butter. I had magazines and books plus anything else which would keep him busy. He had his own phone. Any visitor could come any time. Harold usually met them wearing a sports jacket.

One thing we never saw were bars.

◆ ◆ ◆

If someone other than an athlete could have dominated hockey, it could only be Alan Eagleson. For years he was the voice of international hockey, as well as the NHL.

The Eagle is in eclipse right now, with secret investigations going on questioning the usage of money on Hockey Canada. There is at least one grand jury in Boston looking at this. I have no idea what will happen, but it does seem cruel that they can keep him dangling for almost two years.

I prefer to remember him at the top of his game, thumbing his nose at the entire Russian sports scene, while trying to take over the Ontario Progressive Conservative Party as they prepared to elect a new premier for the province.

Some members of Eagle's law firm "spontaneously" formed a "Friends of Eagleson Club" to see if he could be persuaded to take a run at the premiership. It will surprise no one, I'm sure, to learn that the list of those asked to attend the original meeting was provided to the partners by the Eagle.

Irving Pastermak, senior partner in the law firm, did his best to make it look spontaneous to the group which numbered about thirty-five. Pasty felt the polls were almost even between Al Lawrence and Bill Davis to become the next premier. Eagleson had an ingenious plan to win. He would go to Al Lawrence and ask him to withdraw and ask his delegates to switch to the Eagle.

Amazingly, that was not part of Lawrence's game plan. He declined Eagleson's request and subsequently finished a strong second to Davis.

Davis didn't escape the Eagle's help. Alan, who by now knew he had no chance, went to the premier-to-be and said he'd support him "if you'll lose some weight." I think the only thing Premier Davis lost after his election was Eagleson.

The meeting which was meant to talk the Eagle into the premier's job ended when one of the guests, Bob Bradshaw, a Bay Street Tory, announced: "I'll raise money for you and support you if you'll promise me one thing."

"What's that?" the Eagle inquired.

"You can't use the word shit again until after the campaign," Bradshaw said.

"Shit, Bob." Alan said. "I can't do that."

Meanwhile the Eaglesons and Creightons became good and loyal friends and remain that way today.

One night we invited the Eaglesons for dinner to our place along with the Vic Coulbournes and the Jack Callens. Vic is a Toronto lawyer who bleeds Conservative blue. Jack ran Air Canada in western Canada and liked the Tories also.

Donald, our youngest son, was waiting in the wings for the Eaglesons to arrive. To Don, the Eagle was Santa Claus. Every time he came by the house, Alan brought him some keepsake. That night it was an autographed hockey stick of Darryl Sittler's. The autograph was still damp from the Eagle's pen.

Just before the guests arrived, Donald wanted to know Mrs. Eagleson's first name. "It's Nancy," Marilyn replied, "but Mrs. Eagleson to you."

The dinner was one of those wild affairs, where a lot of wine gets consumed and everyone talks at once. There was no listening. They went home about 2:00 a.m. with Alan still arguing with Nancy.

I was impressed that while the Eagle's profanity was varied and noisy, Nancy seemed to keep up with him nobly.

The next morning Donald woke up Marilyn and me to complain. "You lied to me last night, Mom. You told me Mrs. Eagleson's name was Nancy. It's not — it's shit Nancy."

The Eagle and I like to tell of how we each saved the other's life. I'm very allergic to all nuts and nut oils. He is allergic to crustaceans. There is a kit we each carry that is supposed to be available at all times, in case of emergency.

My problem arose returning from a long weekend in London, England with Roy McMurtry, Jim McCallum, Paul Godfrey, and the Eagle. We'd had a long weekend of gambling, walking, pubbing, *etc.*, and now we were remembering it.

In the long DC 8's that Air Canada used to fly to England, there is a table that seats four situated between the cockpit and the seats. We took it over on take-off and were having a marvellous time reliving the last four days.

A stewardess came along with some cheese with nuts in it which she put on the table. Without thinking, I grabbed a hunk of cheese and wrapped a piece of lettuce around it. I took one bite and instantly felt my throat tingle which was the first sign that it could close. I knew exactly where my emergency kit was — in my other suit packed in the hold. I did the only other thing I could think of. I got sick to my stomach.

By this time my voice had gone. Then I saw the Eagle. He was running up the aisle with his emergency kit, which was the same as mine. It did its job but I felt terrible for the rest of the trip home.

Two weeks later I was having lunch at La Cantinetta with Alan. We were both eating sole. All of a sudden Alan stopped talking, which is unusual for him. I looked at him. His face was breaking out in red dots and his breathing was heavy. "Where is your kit?" I asked. "Back at the office," he gasped.

I examined the sole. It had little hunks of shrimp in the sauce. My secretary, Trudy Eagan, ran down from my office, which was upstairs. She got there just in time. Eagle recently asked that I not tell this story. "They'll know another way to get us!"

During another encounter with Alan, the thought occurred to me that maybe I shouldn't have given him my kit. I was a small shareholder in the Toronto Toros, a hockey team in a league set up by Johnny Bassett. Practically every bright light I knew in the city was involved. You won't find our experience with the Toros in many of our CVs. We bombed spectacularly.

Anyway, that night, we were meeting in Bassett's house to see if we could sign Darryl Sittler, who was represented by the Eagle, and take him from the Leafs — a very important signature because it would prove we were serious and around to stay. We all brought our wives, who entertained Mrs. Sittler while we gave the store away to Darryl. At least I thought we did.

The discussions were amiable and they ended happily. The

conscientious thing to do, the Eagle said, was to let the Leaf management know first so they didn't have to read it in the papers. The Eagle said he'd do that as soon as possible.

However, knowing him, I thought he'd go straight to a phone and call either Milt Dunnell at the Star or George Gross at the Sun, whoever's turn it was for a favour from the Eagle. We all shook hands and departed. We thought this was likely the best deal we'd done since forming the team.

I woke up early the next day and grabbed the Sun. It was Gross's turn. There was the big headline on page one followed by a big story on the lead sports page.

"Leafs Re-sign Sittler in Midnight Meeting.
Beat Toros Offer."

I learned later that the Eagle had arranged to meet King Clancy after our meeting. I phoned him.

"Doesn't a handshake mean a goddamn thing to you?" I asked.

"That's just negotiating," the Eagle said. "You should have signed him when you had him."

I hated my friend for a few months after that. But only a few months. The Eagle is hard to hate.

CHAPTER 7

Sun Rising

Immediately after Bassett's announcement of the closing of the Telegram, the shock waves began to roll. We
were all devastated. So was the city of Toronto.

But a few of us took time to arrange a meeting for
the next evening at Latina, a restaurant on the Queensway.

I told Luigi Orgera, the owner of the restaurant, that nothing of this meeting must leak out. He separated the rest of
Sunday's crowd from us with big floor-to-ceiling walls of
clapboard. I asked him to assign Michael to wait on us
because he couldn't understand English.

(Michael learned English soon enough. He now owns a
highly successful Italian restaurant on Carlton Street named
Barolo. A ten-minute cab ride away, Luigi now owns La
Fenice on King Street, and also cooks for it. In the heady,
early days of the Sun, Luigi, John Bassett and I jointly owned
a restaurant called La Cantinetta. We're happy we kept our
day jobs.)

The announcement came a month before the actual closing. It gave us only a few weeks to start a paper. Although
we had not raised any money, with that time frame, we knew
we had to plan as if we had.

Don Hunt, Worthington, and I were at all the subsequent series of planning meetings. We picked the minds of several others, already committed to the project. How long they could remain committed was a big question.

Other Canadian newspapers looking for good staffers were interviewing daily, and not only in Toronto. There were so many Tely people available that interviewers talked to you only once. If you hesitated, the interviewer was on to the next person. You wouldn't hear back again.

That put plenty of pressure on Tely staffers to make commitments to other papers. The first sign that we might have a popular idea with our new tabloid was that only three out of sixty-two people we wanted opted to take a guaranteed job. The rest took a wild gamble on a tabloid with no name and no money. We had at least captured their imaginations.

Worthington became the secretary to our group and wrote down our plans, our dreams, our hopes and our emerging notion of what kind of paper we might produce. All this without the benefit of the ubiquitous surveys we have today. It didn't take long for the little group that met at Latina to figure out we were sailing into uncharted seas. But we did our jobs well.

Firstly, we had our current jobs only until the end of October. The Tely was sinking, but virtually all its employees were now working together to make sure that we produced a good product until the end. We were going at it like the pros we were. Ironically, a lot of those who worked so hard and with such pride in those last days had voted for the strike that put the final nail in the Tely's coffin.

Secondly, we weren't sure what to do. None of us had ever rented a building, found a press, bought newsprint or started a company. Hardly any of us had dummied a tabloid paper before.

It has been argued that every successful enterprise requires three leaders; a dreamer, a businessman and a son of a bitch. Well, we had all three in Hunt, Worthington and myself. I'll leave it to the reader to fit us into the proper category.

Our initial search for money in early October failed so miserably that we abandoned the project and dispatched our group.

Day-oners

No book written about the Sun would be complete without naming our originals. I believe in every case they turned down another job to go for the brass ring. Here they are:

Ken Adachi, George Anthony, Frank Benedetti, Norm Betts, Ray Biggart, David Black, Christina Blizzard, Linda Bone, Bruce Borland, Kathy Brooks, Helen Bourke, James Brown, Mary Buchanan, Larry Collins, Olive Collins, Dave Cooper, Kaye Corbett, Ron Cornell, James Cowan, Jeff Crawford, Doug Creighton, Sandra D'Cruz, Andy Donato, John Downing, Frank Eames, Graham Evoy, Domenica Farella, David Farrer, Mike Farrugia, Doug Fisher, Hugh Funston, Paul Gillespie, George Gross, William Hay, Howard Hayes, Art Holland, Jac Holland, Eaton Howitt, Don Hunt, John Iaboni, Noel Ing, Gordon Jackson, Sherry Johnston, John Jursa, Margaret Kmiciewicz, Bill King, Wasyl Kowalishen, John LeMay, Bob MacDonald, John MacKay, Grant Maxwell, Mike McCabe, Bob McMillan, Cal Millar, Norm Milne, Ed Monteith, Michelle Morey, Bill Nicholson, Maury Nicholson, Don Nixon, Jean Osborne, Dick Plummer, Bruce Rae, Ann Rankin, Ted Reeve, Dennis Ricker, Paul Rimstead, Ken Robertson, Bob Routledge, Dick Shatto, Joan Sutton, Jim Thomson, Donnie Tonks, Ron Tonks, Sylvia Train, Bruce Tuttle, Ed Tybruczyk, Jim Walsh, Glen Woodcock, Peter Worthington, Jim Yates, Mary Zelezinsky.

We had (and preferred) a proposal from lawyer Eddie Hyde. He was willing to put up $300,000 and go it alone. That wasn't enough but it was a long way from our first meeting at the Latina. He had telephoned out of the blue after a brief huddle with a mutual friend Daryl Wells, who called the races at Woodbine.

Hyde ran a small financial daily report on bankruptcies. All he wanted from us initially was to see if he could somehow add a page of sports coverage to our new paper.

We met at the Walker House and, by the time he left, the one page had become a whole paper. Meanwhile, others were on the hunt for money as well.

Fraser Kelly, political editor of the Telegram, who wasn't even coming with us in the venture, discovered that Stanley Randall, a former provincial cabinet minister, was an entrepreneur. Worthington interviewed Stephen Roman and, when he was finished, recommended we say no because he thought that Roman might use the paper to promote his own news too much.

On October 7th, we threw in the sponge in Eddie Hyde's boardroom. Jack Daniels, who ran Cadillac Fairview at the time, had been recruited by Eddie Goodman, his lawyer, who was also present.

Stan Randall sat with Hyde. Then came the four financial dummies — Hunt, Worthington, Andy MacFarlane and myself. We were, by this time, wed to starting the day after the Tely's demise on October 31st. That drove the financial experts to distraction.

"You have to have the money yesterday," Daniels said. "It will take two weeks."

I shot the Hyde alone deal down reluctantly. "We need more than $300,000," I said.

Andy MacFarlane, my predecessor as managing editor at the Tely, put his hat on and walked from the deal forever. Worthington followed, leaving Hunt and me alone. We realized, finally, that we were dead in the water. We shook hands and left. We were devastated.

We stopped briefly at the Telegram to tell the people who had agreed to come with us to look elsewhere. In frustration, we adjourned to the Walker House and cried in our beer for an hour or so.

When we were leaving, we decided to head to Port Elgin with our wives the next day, if the good weather hung in. We didn't want to spend the next few days talking about a newspaper that, except for lack of financing, we knew we could make work.

Totally unknown to us, as we skipped rocks into Lake Huron the next day, Worthington back in Toronto was still in the business of raising money. He decided to try Goodman again. This time Eddie had enough positive responses to convince Peter he should call us in Port Elgin.

Easier said than done. We didn't have a phone, and Peter had no idea of who else he could call.

"Is there a bakery in town?" he asked the operator, remembering I had raved to him about the fresh dinner rolls.

"One," the operator said, "Bolander's Bakery."

"Try it," Worthington told her. By chance he'd found our landlord, Ella Bolander.

Ella showed up at our place and minutes later, I was standing in the middle of warm rolls and bread listening to Worthington, who was telling me: "Eddie thinks he can get us a million dollars." It was just what we needed to hear. We didn't sleep that night, and left for Toronto the next day.

Cool, calm and collected, we went to see Goodman on Sunday night. Eddie had indeed nailed down most of the million for us and we were on again, this time with no turning back. It was a real Thanksgiving holiday, but we had precious little time left to get up and running.

We now knew we had some money at least. Enough, probably, to keep us for a couple of months. I'm sure no one will ever again start a daily newspaper in a major city on such a shoestring. (The Edmonton and Calgary start-ups lost money for four years before achieving profitability.)

The arguments raged in earnest now in our group over the sort of paper we'd start and the date of our first edition. Don

Don, We Miss You

Don Nixon died while I was finishing this book. He and Dougie Payne were our original cleaners at the Eclipse building. They were full-time but were classified by the financial wizards as "full-time, part-time."

I always hated the designation, which was used, I think, mainly to avoid paying benefits.

Dougie Payne died several years ago. Don stayed with us and became permanent staff. We backdated his full-time appointment to day one so he had the benefits as well as the shares (1,300) given to each day-oner.

Don never sold a Sun share until he retired. Then he bought the first house he ever owned. Don was a shining example of what we visualized in the beginning for Sun employees. Everyone with an opportunity for a piece of the action.

The day after Don retired, he returned to the Sun to work delivering advertising proofs. No doubt, somewhere in the human resources department was a "full-time, part-time" card.

Day one re-created at our twentieth anniversary celebration. We concluded we hadn't aged.

Our twentieth anniversary party at Sky Dome.

The Big Four — from left to right: Myself, Hunt, Worthington and Dunlop.
We learned from each other.

Photo Credit: Ottmar Bierwagon

Left: With Jim Bowes (founder of Bowes Publishing), one minute from getting richer.

Below: Walter Cronkite — he did for network news what we tried to do in newspapers.

Lord Creighton of Winston's and Lord Thomson of Fleet surround John Bassett.

The Order of Canada. April 29, 1992 — my finest hour was soon to be replaced by my worst.

Two world class organizers with world class counsellor. From left to right: Lynn Carpenter, Jim McCallum, Annemarie Cimowsky.

The Order of Canada. April 29, 1992 — my finest hour was soon to be replaced by my worst.

Two world class organizers with world class counsellor.
From left to right: Lynn Carpenter, Jim McCallum,
Annemarie Cimowsky.

Gorby, Mila and Doug. Gorby and I have one thing in common — we were both overthrown.

Above: A moment in my life, singing *Danny Boy* with the Cardinal. He doesn't sound as good as John McDermott, but he makes more sense.

Right: Vanessa Harwood, holding the first birthday edition.

Above left: King Clancy, everyone's friend. He would have loved the 1992-93 hockey season.

Above right: My hero Ed Mirvish and his wife Ann. They are Toronto.

The prime minister looking far too happy, considering he was with two publishers. It's my belief Brian will go down in history as one of Canada's best prime ministers. I think he took the hard decisions.

The prime minister said to me, "I'll take *my* tie and *your* balance sheet."

Photo Credit: Jeff Bassett

Left: With Jim Bowes (founder of Bowes Publishing), one minute from getting richer.

Below: Walter Cronkite — he did for network news what we tried to do in newspapers.

Lord Creighton of Winston's and Lord Thomson of Fleet surround John Bassett.

Driver and friend Mike McCabe, his new wife Sharon, plus new driver.

Howard "Billard" and I with a Donato cartoon. Yes, yes; I know it's Harold Ballard. Despite all his shortcomings, he sure helped me out when I joined the sports department.

The directors in happier days. From left to right, back row — Rudy Bratty; Paul Beeston; *Calgary Sun* publisher Ken King; chief financial officer Bruce Jackson; Frank King; *Toronto Sun* publisher Jim Tighe; associate publisher in Calgary Craig Martin; *Edmonton Sun* publisher Ron Mitchell; Herb Solway; Paul Godfrey. Front row — Washington bureau chief Patrick Harden; Lionel Schipper; my executive assistant Lynn Carpenter; secretary to the board Kim Seto; previous Canadian ambassador Derek Burney (this photo was taken on the roof of the Canadian Embassy in Washington); me; *Ottawa Sun* publisher Hartley Steward; my secretary extraordinarie Chris Young; Ron Osbourne; Trudy Eagan; and Don Campbell.

My family. From left to right, front row — Marilyn Creighton, Terry Keough-Creighton, Alex Creighton, Sarah Creighton, Laura Creighton. Middle row — Bruce Creighton, James Creighton, Donald Creighton, Ann Creighton, Sandy Creighton, Christine Creighton. Back row — David Creighton, Scott Creighton, Doug Creighton.

Hunt and I were in favour of going to press twenty-four hours after the Tely went down. Fourteen of our group voted to delay the start-up. The tally was 14-2 for delay.

So we suspended democracy for a brief time, as we would do now and then over the next twenty years, and planned for an immediate start after the Tely's final edition. We would go November 1, 1971.

Bob MacMillan, our news editor, found and rented the building. It was downtown on King Street West and was called the Eclipse building — a fine name for a building in which to start a newspaper called the *Toronto Sun*. Our second floor space would not be ready for the first edition, so we moved temporarily to the fourth floor. The building was unbelievably cold, because someone had knocked a hole in the back wall to bring in a large machine, and it had never been fixed.

In our many meetings at Latina, our group discussed in great detail the newspaper we wanted to give birth to. The arguments ebbed and flowed, but there were many points of agreement. In the end, we had a pretty fair notion of the Sun we wanted. Perhaps some of our original notes from those meetings might be of interest. They were taken in October of 1971 by Peter Worthington.

Name
Problem is to create a tabloid free from the prejudice that's usually associated with tabloids, *e.g.* Flash, Hush, *etc.* A respectable news/feature/pix tabloid requires traditional newspaper name. One that fits with Toronto's galaxy newspapers, Star, Globe, *etc.* is *Toronto Sun* — "Toronto's Other Voice." (I think the name was Donato's contribution.)

Why a Tabloid?

With the demise of the Telegram a vacuum exists. Also considerable emotionalism prevalent over loss of Tely, which tabloid could exploit and capture. (We tried but mostly failed.)

We feel that Toronto is "ripe" for a tabloid — even before Tely's death. A solid potential tabloid staff available with Tely going; also have access to Tely library and record room (thanks to John Bassett), which essential to provide necessary "depth" for a serious newspaper (otherwise forced to be superficial); also chance to buy 2,200 Tely "boxes", plus chance to pick up Tely ads, which now up for grabs.

Star's advertising rates have jumped nine percent, with further jump totalling twenty-three percent expected in January; means that a large segment of business community can't afford Star prices. Whole new advertising market exists for good tabloid.

Why Morning Tabloid?

The Globe is most vulnerable — street sales total about 55,000 and delivery 65,000. The Globe is dull. ROB is good. Blanket the subways each day.

Go in the morning — costs are lower. Fewer staff, better rates for distributing, only one printing per day. If p.m.: have to fight Star, several editions, bigger staff, around-the-clock work, more vulnerability. Price — ten cents: Star expected to go to fifteen cents in New Year.

Editorial Policy

Important to be different from other two papers. Policy would be of basic "independence" and ideologically in the centre — more so than either Globe or Star. It would appeal basically to people who work for a living, not those who seek a free ride from society.

It would concentrate on local affairs — would be brightly written, irreverent, but balanced and responsible. In essence, it would tend to be an "opposition" newspaper and have no sacred cows. It would be the mouthpiece of no group — and certainly not the fashionable "left" elements of our society.

The editorials would be straight, hard-hitting and opinionated, and quite unlike the wishy-washy editorials that the Telegram indulged in. They'd be *Daily Mirror*-style in bluntness. We would stress the idea that we are Toronto's "other voice" — the voice that the death of the Tely deprived Torontonians of. Keep stressing our independence. (That policy was exactly what we had to have and what we got from Peter.)

Contents

A newspaper of opinionated news, there'd be a variety of columnists, ranging from Bill Buckley to Tiny Bennett. The stress would be hard on sports, starting from back towards centre of paper —Jim Coleman, Jim Murray columns, plus pix and local sports. Aimed at men on morning commuter runs. (We had a big fight here. Worthington wanted sports on the back page and Hunt and I wanted to sell ads on it. Money triumphed. Worthington quit for the first time, but was back twenty-four hours later.)

Heavy on women's stuff — Joan Sutton's page, complete with Dear Abby, Horoscope, Irma Bombeck column, *etc.*, along with entertainment page, George Anthony, gossip columns, Susan Ford, Earl Wilson and the like.

(The Sun would also take over Telegram syndicate service which, without Telegram, earns some $30,000 profit a year.)

News columns laced with pictures, short items, all bright and even cheeky without losing balance. Columns would follow the Telegram edict of "freedom" to columnist, regardless of views, on the theory that freedom of press not only freedom to express a certain strong editorial policy, but also freedom of reader to have access to individual opinion.

He Is Such a Nice Guy

Garth Drabinsky is, in my view, the most brilliant art promoter in Canada. He was commenting on the Sun at a Variety Club lunch honouring the late Edward Dunlop, the Sun's first president.

He said: "The Sun is a tremendous power for good. And a watchdog checking on those who govern us at every level. He is a supporter of worthy causes, and we should pause after I finish to take account of how greatly we'd despair without it."

Method of Operation

Keep capital expenditures low, therefore to own little and rent everything — desks, typewriters, presses, *etc.*

Important to pay good, competitive wages to staff, and eventually get strong, loyal, able staff.

No union, therefore important to eventually get some sort of profit-sharing system, or share-option system for staff. Can't start off on this, but when profits become reasonable, important to raise wages even beyond that of other papers.

Have to be prepared to guarantee some job security to employees, in that the paper should be prepared to try and survive for at least a year so employees can be assured of that much.

Management
Unstructured, with journalists in essence running the show and determining editorial policy in a loose-knit way, in cooperation with the financial backers. The principals prepared to do a variety of work, all contributing towards putting out a tough, professional product that will appeal to working people.

Circulation
Think modest is the key, and better to under-estimate than over-estimate. Circulation, under normal circumstances should settle at about 50,000 from TTC and street sales. If we can get into apartments and get hotels to buy and distribute, should result in sales reaching 75,000 quite quickly. Advertising revenue seems solid, especially if we can get into apartments.

(Well, it was a little low.)

General
In summation, the proposed *Toronto Sun* does not see itself as a rival to either Globe or Star, but simply filling a vacuum that exists and which the other papers are not filling.

Aggressive, the Sun would be hard to fight. If the Star tries to swamp it by starting a morning tabloid too, to fight it on those grounds and to take the fight to the people who've already had one voice crushed by the Star. By remaining unintimidated, aggressive, accurate and irreverent, the Sun becomes hard to fight and the big papers suddenly have the appearance of being "bullies" if they put pressure on.

The newpaper has the appearance of "continuity" from the dead Tely, without being the Telegram. It becomes an unavoidable news story and human interest story in its own right, with the romantic idea of a bunch of journalists trying to keep an independent voice for the people. You can't be ignored, and the promotional aspects are unavoidable and intriguing.

When we started the *Toronto Sun* in 1971, our entire staff was out of work, albeit for only a day. We were poor and although some of our directors had lots of money, very little of it was at the Sun. Our investors were there only thanks to Eddie Goodman.

No one had started a major daily in decades, so it was a great turn-on. We were under-financed and hungry. More importantly, our morale was wonderful.

CHAPTER 8

Sunburst

I t was 3:00 a.m.
Inside Inland Publishing was a group of well-dressed, newly-minted directors of the *Toronto Sun*, Canada's newest daily newspaper. The food trays were empty, the booze put away long ago, the ice which chilled the champagne had melted.

They were all there because Eddie Goodman had put the arm on them to invest in this wild scheme for a new newspaper. He had warned them they were not likely to get a dime back. They were beginning to believe him. And they wanted to know why they were still cooling their heels at this ungodly hour of the morning.

The sixty-two happy staffers at the Sun had long ago lost their happy smiles and were now looking desperate.

The Urbanite press which was to have started at ll:00 p.m. was motionless. Part of the problem was a lost courier on his way from the King Street Sun offices to the Oakville printing plant. A column had been left at the Sun. Nonetheless, shortly before 1:00 a.m., the paper had been ready to roll.

But the press still hadn't started. There were those who wondered if were possible to fail without ever publishing a paper. Suddenly, gloriously, a bell sounded and the press began to turn over. The pressman who got it going said: "I don't know what I did."

Whatever, there it was, the first Sun slipping along the delivery belt. Douglas Bassett ran over and gave me the first one and handed Marilyn and me two glasses of warm champagne. It was the best drink we ever had.

There would be more start-ups in the future (and more press problems), but there would never be another moment like this. There wasn't a dry eye in the place.

The Sun was alive!

Outside, fifteen impatient wholesalers were threatening to go home. The guy who calmed them down was another wholesaler, Dennis Ricker, who has now led his group for longer than I have.

Dennis' background had been in unions, but now he was an entrepreneur. Other entrepreneurs are lucky that Dennis waited as long as he did. He has been a wholesaler extraordinaire.

While the trucks were loading, the staff of the Sun stood watching and wishing them well. Suddenly, the significance of the moment

Figures For All

I had lunch at the York Club with Floyd Chalmers, honourary chairman of Maclean Hunter. Chalmers was partially deaf and wanted to know the six month figures for the Sun. I had to shout them for him to hear.

On the way out, I nodded at Beland Honderich, chairman of the Star and Don McGiverin, governor of the Bay. McGiverin later phoned to say they enjoyed our figures and could I do it again every six months. This would allow Honderich to replace the accountant he had tracking the Sun's performance.

seemed to hit like an emotional storm. Everyone was shaking hands and hugging everyone else. They reminded me of a family. In a remarkable moment, everybody reached out. Ours is a fairly cynical business, and that just doesn't happen. I realized that I had tears again. I snuck away, knowing we couldn't miss.

Meanwhile, the boys at the long bar at the Lord Simcoe Hotel were running a pool on how many weeks we would last. But I knew we were going to surprise a lot of people with our product. We had the talent.

We had the best of Tely photographers in Norm Betts, Jac Holland, and Dave Cooper.

We had John Downing at City Hall who outwrote and outscooped the five-man Star bureau.

We had Joan Sutton, perhaps as good an example as any of the innovative use of talent made by our fledgling newspaper. She had only a few months in our business when we hired her to be a featured columnist. This would never happen at the establishment papers. She wrote emotionally and powerfully and she was a megahit with Sun readers.

Joan was totally involved with the Sun. With her husband Oscar's help, she managed to get past the front door of people who just didn't do interviews, especially with fledgling tabs. Once she got near them, however, she made them talk far more openly than I'm sure they thought they would.

The entrees, in some cases, were helped along by Oscar, who is a well-known and well-connected American financier. Marilyn and I first met him at Joan's small, restored home on Metcalfe Street in downtown Toronto. At the time I doubted Oscar had ever been in a home that small. I was wrong. He is a modest person, a man's man, an ardent fisherman and sailor who also shoots, gardens and cooks. He is also in love with Joan.

That evening he was attempting to put us all at ease. "It's snowing outside," said Oscar to no one's surprise. "Why don't I light us a fire?" I noticed earlier that it had been carefully prepared.

We found out how hard it was snowing a minute or two later because we were standing in it. Oscar had forgotten to open the damper.

He is gracious and helpful about Joan's career although I'm sure he'd rather have her to himself. At a company seminar in New York, he once pulled me aside to hit me up for a raise for Joan.

A few years later, we were all at a party for Ed Asner of *Lou Grant* fame who had come from his Los Angeles home to be our city editor for a day.

I guess there was some drinking going on because the ever-present Rimstead whispered: "Let's give them some fun." He pushed Joan to the floor and proceeded to simulate a sex act.

Although I didn't see this or hear of it until I got back to the office, Joan, who was terribly embarrassed and upset, demanded I apologize on behalf of the paper. Rimstead merely felt it was fun shared with Joan.

Joan and I met for lunch at Winston's and stupidly painted ourselves into a corner we shouldn't have gotten ourselves into. To my horror, she quit. Hartley Steward, who was managing editor of the Star at the time, immediately contacted her and hired her.

Later David Peterson, premier at the time, hired her as the Ontario representative for New York. When Bob Rae moved in he was too much for Joan. Me too. So we were together again.

The columns she wrote about my firing by the board made Marilyn and me cry. It took a brave employee to write those columns. Who would have thought she'd end up at the Star again?

To confound the odds for the boys at the Simcoe bar, our young paper, of course, had the Rimmer. Paul was a former sports writer and general columnist for the Telegram.

He really was an extraordinary columnist and journalist, and an amazing character. From the first day of publication he made real for us our daily miracle. Somehow, through his

Rimmer Wins a Bet

Rimstead and I were going to a Blue Jays game one evening. We were meeting for a pre-game drink at the Le Cantinetta at 7:00 p.m. When I arrived, he was asleep at the table. The Rimmer had met his love, Ms. Hinkey, for lunch and simply stayed on to meet me.

He was hammered.

He told me he still had to write his column for the next day. I could see we were not likely to get to the ball game.

"I'll file it now," he lisped. "Have a drink and I'll be with you in a minute." Nonsense, I thought, and told him it was impossible to do a column in ten minutes.

I offered to bet twenty dollars he couldn't do it. He accepted.

He dialled his editor. There wasn't a piece of paper in sight.

Eight minutes later he returned to the table. "Okay, let's go to the ball game."

I paid him the next day. His column was about running into me and betting me twenty dollars that he could write a column in less than ten minutes.

columns, we came to know who we were. He pushed the limits of newspapering for us and taught us all that newspapers need not be as boring and dry as the traditional broadsheet papers.

He chronicled in his column our trials and errors. He characterized us as a band of hard-working, fun-loving newspaper people hell-bent on starting and keeping alive an alternative newspaper in Toronto. He had it right. We didn't always know what we were doing, but we were game and hardy. Maybe foolhardy. Rimstead made amazing contact with his readers and he sold us and our paper to them. He got one letter addressed to him at the Sun — "Next door to Farb's Car Wash, Across from the Kingsplate Open Kitchen, A long way west from the Globe and the Star, part of the fourth floor with Tailabelts Co."

The mailman certainly knew us.

A few days after we started, advertising director Bruce Tuttle posted a note on our bulletin board listing the daily circulation of the three Toronto papers:

Toronto Star 271,000
Globe and Mail 126,000
Toronto Sun .... 76,480 (first day)
.... 124,940 (second day)
.... 127,800 (third day)

Rimstead checked the figures with me. I said I didn't know what the actual sale was because our distributors only picked up the unsold papers weekly.

On the first day, the presses were three hours late starting, so we only printed 75,000 papers. The second and third days we printed just less than 125,000. According to Tuttle we were selling just slightly more than we were printing. Which is some feat.

Rimstead told me Tuttle's numbers, then wrote the whole thing for our readers.

Rimstead, who said he drank to make other people more interesting, wrote just before he died: "I owe much ... I have nothing ... the rest I leave to the poor."

The first day Rimstead came to the office he plugged in his kettle to make a pot of tea and blew a fuse. Then he heard the elevator had stuck and that George Gross had to get to his office by climbing up the elevator cable.

He immediately blamed our landlord, Jack Diamond, a brilliant young architect, for the whole thing. The incorrigible Rimmer called him our slum landlord.

Rimmer asked readers to come and have a look at the place for themselves, while we were putting out a paper. To our astonishment, over 8,000 of them turned up, for a tour led by several of us. But Rimstead one-upped us by bringing a date — Miss May from *Playboy* magazine.

Paul represented a part of society that regular people seldom meet. In a real way and, in the spirit of fun, he created a brief period of escape from reality.

He died young, as we expected. Of course, all of us who knew him are touched with dozens of good memories of him.

My last conversation with him was on the phone. I was in my office and Paul was in a hospital bed in Florida, from which he then knew he would never emerge alive.

He kept telling me he wanted to be judged by his writing, not his personality. This struck me as odd, because his writing had his personality riveted all through it.

We reminisced about Paul's wish to write a book in Mexico. He had moved there after a couple of months with the Sun to fulfil a dream of writing a great work of fiction.

Of course, he went broke in Mexico and had to call for help. Some people thought I was nasty, but I got him back by wiring his pay each payday to a town about 600 miles north of where he was.

He thought he got even about a year later when I was speaking to a combined junior and senior board of trade meeting. I learned at the last minute that he was to introduce me.

"Look at publisher Creighton's suit," he said. "He paid $900 for it at Harry Rosen's and it looks great on him. I paid $1,000 for mine from the same tailor. The only reason I can think of why he looks so much better than I do is that he must take his off before he goes to bed."

Then he called on me. He was a difficult act to follow.

There was a moment of magic at the Eclipse building when the Telegram's great sports columnist, Ted Reeve, with hundreds of readers in tow, we knew, turned up to begin writing his wonderful column for us. The whole staff stood up and applauded.

"I keep getting the feeling I'm writing for *La Petite Journal*," he wrote. "I set the typewriter by the door so the carriage can go into the newsroom on longer sentences."

Who knew the workings of our federal government better than Doug Fisher? He was our man in Ottawa. And the boys at the Simcoe underestimated his appeal as well.

Worthington produced editorial pages read by more people than any other page in the paper, something you likely can't say of any other newspaper in Canada.

Donato is simply the best cartoonist in Canada. He always

draws me either with a martini in hand or my shirt collar popped up. He was offended when the board got me so he kindly worked in a drawing of me every day. It's still going as I write this.

George Gross produced the best sports pages in Canada.

Creative people tend to make their problems everyone's problems. But I thought it was always worthwhile to cater to them. How I miss them now.

I believed sincerely that if we could publish it and deliver it, we were going to make it. Because we had the goods. We had our own stars and own characters and they would attract and keep readers.

◆ ◆ ◆

One of the best moves the Sun board made was the appointment of Edward Dunlop as the first president of the Sun.

He was to be the directors' and investors' link to Sun management. Originally the board and the investors wanted to appoint the chief financial officer, who would then report to the board rather than to Don Hunt and me.

We said "no way." Edward was the compromise. The board couldn't have selected a finer gentleman or a more productive mind.

Edward was a true Canadian hero. He was finally awarded the Order of Canada the day before he died from cancer in 1981.

He won the George Cross and lost his sight shortly before D-Day. A young soldier training for the invasion froze with a live grenade in his hand. Edward grabbed it and pushed him to the ground. In saving the youngster's life, Edward took the blast himself. Besides being blinded permanently, he also lost two fingers.

10 Reasons Why the Sun Shines

By *Christie Blatchford*
November 1, 1991 - Twentieth Anniversary Edition

I am not a Sun original. I had to work my way up from the *Globe and Mail* (which is a good place for a young journalist to begin, being as serious and self-important as most young journalists) and the *Toronto Star* (where one can be almost as serious, but get paid better).

I have, however, been at the Sun for almost a decade, which is twice as long as I have ever stayed anywhere else. What follows, with due kudos to David Letterman who did this first, is "My Top 10 Reasons For Coming To The Sun - And Why I Have Stayed So Long":

10. The Sunshine Girl.
First, the page three girl allows me to keep track of what happens to cheerleaders when they get old enough to vote. Second, I like the idea that it frankly offends major-league feminists, whom I find offensive. Finally, it keeps photographers on the streets and out of the office, where they would only get in trouble.

9. No union.
It's not that I am anti-union, it's that I am anti-union for newspaper writers. Newspaper writers need leashes, if they need anything, not unions. This is one of the greatest jobs in the world. I do not need a union to tell me I should also be demanding time-and-a-half while I am seeing something interesting, staying in a hotel, and eating at company expense.

8. Easy to Read.
Yeah, yeah, everyone says it. But I don't mean I like the paper because it is a tabloid and therefore easily foldable while standing in a subway car (though this is true and it is handier for the bathtub). The Sun is easy to read because, as a tab, it demands of its writers brevity and clarity.

Sometimes, our stories are better simply because the writer was not allowed to ramble on and on. This is not always true, but it is more often than not.

7. Sex appeal.

Let's face it, the Sun is a sexy newspaper. I don't know what makes a paper sexy, but I know what doesn't, and what isn't. The Globe is sometimes sexy, and the Star is almost never sexy, and we are often sexy.

6. No women's caucus.

Both the Globe and the Star have women's caucuses, groups of very serious and high-minded women who meet regularly to complain about men getting the better assignments. I am a low-minded woman. If I were to form a similar group here at the Sun, the name of the group would sound the same, but it would be spelled differently, if you get my drift, and if you are low-minded, you do.

5. Paul Rimstead.

The Rimmer has been gone a long while now, but in the early days of the paper, when he was still flying, he was fun to read and sometimes much more than that. He was also a character. In a world where even sports reporters now work out regularly - what they used to do was drink out - and characters are few and far between, he was a treasure.

4. Joan Sutton.

She used to drive me crazy as a reader, her and those crazy love-and-feelings columns she wrote. I often wrote what I thought were incredibly clever parodies of her column. Only later did I realize that I never missed it, that I always read the sucker. Only much, much later did I realize this was all that mattered.

3. The parties.

Once, when I was still at the Star, I was invited by Pat Hickey, then working at the Sun, to a huge Sun party, held, I think, at the Old Mill. It was an amazing evening. People drank and danced to excess, ate like pigs and howled like dogs. There were at least two good fistfights, one of which involved at least a dozen people. Coming from a mining town in the wilds of Quebec, where people did this all winter, I felt immediately at home.

2. Limited middle management.
Though the paper has put on a few pounds in this particular area of late, the ranks of those whose jobs are mysteries to the rest of us are still thin, especially by comparison to One Yonge, where, if you wanted to see a story through to the bitter end, you would see it pass through about thirty-one hands, be completely rewritten four times, and be scheduled for pages as diverse as the front and the comic page. This kind of stuff doesn't happen because of editors, but because of middle managers. It doesn't happen often at the Sun, where tolerance is, rightly, still limited for such things as focus groups, management by objectives, and the like.

1. Doug Creighton.
Then and now, the glue who holds the joint together, gives great parties, is loyal to old ideas but open to new ones, calls them as he sees them. It's an honor to work for him, and you know that comes around only once in a lifetime, if you're lucky. I am.

For some it would be the end of a productive life. Not for Edward. He married his part-time nurse, Dorrie, whom he had never seen. They raised two children. After the war, Edward entered politics and became a cabinet minister in the Robarts' government. He sat on the CRTC board, was a governor on the board of the University of Toronto, and ran the Canadian Arthritis Society until his death.

Originally, I thought we might have hit the *Guinness Book of World Records* before we printed a paper.

How many newspapers in the world had a blind president,

I thought. My scepticism soon disappeared. I wound up travelling with Edward, going to the theatre and movies with him and even the odd Blue Jay game. The more time I spent with him the more respect I gained for this extraordinary man.

He made the people with him make him see. Surely it is one of the ultimate tests of a reporter to write in a way so enduring their readers see what is being written about.

His concerns for those in the shadows of life, his demands for excellence and his constant desire to know more, all worked together to make those of us who produced the Sun in those days better journalists.

I knew very quickly that we had the right man in the right job. Edward was being driven through Rosedale on his way home by Michael McCabe, who eventually became my long-time driver. (Mike actually carries business cards describing himself as director of fleet maintenance.)

Mike was lost and trying not to admit it. "You don't know where you are Michael," said Edward. "What intersection are we at?" Michael told him. "Turn right here, then left two blocks down, then right again at the next intersection and you're on our street." Edward was right, and McCabe has never lived it down.

A few weeks later, Marilyn and I went to Vienna for

Can You See Your Way Clear

Edward Dunlop checked into Calgary's Westin Hotel. "There's no bed in my room," he complained.

"Are you blind or something? Oh my God, you are," said the receptionist. Nonetheless, there was no bed in the room.

a week. Dorrie and Edward, by coincidence, were also there. They had been in Vienna four times, but all of them since he was blinded. We'd never been.

He took us on a half-mile walk to the Coursalon Park to a restaurant where they played Viennese waltzes. That done, he took us back a different way.

It was shortly after that that Edward cemented our relationship forever. We were meeting once a month and Edward suggested we might do this over lunch at Winston's Restaurant, preceded by a martini, after which I would read Edward the menu while he pretended not to know it off by heart. He was just creating more time to order a second martini.

We would order it while the food was coming. Once, he asked for corned beef hash, which, I must say, is tough to get at Winston's. Needless to say we had a third drink while waiting for it. That meant Edward ordered corned beef hash from then on because he always set the afternoon aside for the Sun discussion.

Finally, by arrangement with John Arena, I pre-ordered the corned beef hash so that it arrived with our first drink. Edward, always a gentlemen, said: "Douglas, you are a son of a bitch," and never ordered corned beef hash again.

Edward was a perfectionist and he persisted until we finally succeeded. He always thought we could write and edit better than we did. I miss him and so does the Sun.

It's The People, Not The Place

By J. Douglas Creighton
Speech at Twentieth Anniversary Party

It is twenty years, as you know, since I first spoke to the original Sun staff. The time, the place, and a lot of the people are different. But there was something then that is present now. You're not issued with it, you can't buy it, or be awarded it. It is the spirit of the Sun. And it is great!

It is the leadership and dedication of the likes of Monteith, Gross, Webb, Jackson, Pyette, Steward and many others that inspires the loyalty and dedication of their staffs.

It is the energy, brains and strong will of Worthington; the bombast and tenacity of Hunt; the creativity of MacMillan; the wonderful, brash humor of Rimstead and Dunford; the artistic genius of Donato. The way he draws, if he weren't a cartoonist, he'd be an assassin. It is the parties where we carry on like members of the closest family, and it is the will to win by all our departments.

It is the National Newspaper and Dunlop Awards we've won and circulation and advertising records we've set; it's Blatchford's amazing, descriptive ability - leaving out some of the profanity; it's the transformation from the Eclipse building to today's terrific new quarters.

The Sun's Board of Directors, as it should, casts a huge shadow of influence over our company.

In any business, the company can buy a person's time and ensure their physical presence at a given location. But, as I indicated earlier, you cannot buy loyalty or devotion to the job. You must earn that. Team spirit gives us the edge over our opposition. Our board knows and supports this. They also know that for a beginning business to earn a place in the Sun, it has to put up with a few blisters.

Our board has always felt close to our employees.

It was led initially by Edward Dunlop. Edward was never a journalist, but he had an impact on the Sun greater than many of us. He made people with him see and surely that is one of the ultimate tests of a good reporter.

One of my favorite sports columnists, Red Smith, once wrote in his *New York Times* column: "Too many damned newspapers retire too damned many guys at seventy and too few at twenty-five. They should keep the good ones as long as they can perform." He might have been writing about John Grant, Jim McCallum and Fred Metcalf. Their geniality, sense of humor and continued caring were a great benefit to our company, and we miss them!

The rest of us now sit in our new boardroom. This is where everyone talks, no one listens, and when it's all over, everyone disagrees.

In any organization there is, regrettably, death. Not many, thank God, but we have lost Edward Dunlop, Ted Reeve (alias "the Moaner"), Jimmy Richards, Ross McLaughlin, Val Bird, Paul Rimstead, Bob Pennington and others. Thank you for being remarkable. Thank you for having the vision that made all this possible. Together, we shared our successes. The hard part is now - without you.

I've always thought a chief executive's role should be that of a caretaker, as well as a leader. To make sure the company balance sheet is in good shape, and make sure successors are in place. But, just as important, to ensure the employees are better, happier and richer. We've tried. We're proud, but only the staff knows the answer.

We know at the Sun you must take risks to get what you want in life. When there is no risk, there is no pride in achievement. We've taken a lot of risks at the Sun and beaten the odds. The company is still growing, still young and facing new challenges.

Bear Bryant, the famous football coach at Alabama, had a philosophy I agree with. He used to say: "If anything goes bad, I did it. If anything goes good, we did it. If anything goes real good, then you did it."

Well, we at the Sun did it. It's been a great twenty years!

CHAPTER 9

Sunday Finally Works

By the time we'd completed a full year of daily Suns, it occurred to Hunt and me that we should be looking at a Sunday paper.

We were confident that the Globe had nothing in the works but the Star was, we were sure, constantly reviewing the situation. It was likely that, being big and ponderous and unionized, they would take several months to respond. What we were privately concerned about was what would happen if we were initially successful and the Star countered by moving the contents of their massive Saturday paper to Sunday. A ridiculous concern, some said. Why would they put at risk the biggest newspaper and money-spinner in Canada?

Finally, we decided to sneak up on them and do it. First it required proper promotion, extra staff, including an editor, and, of course, board approval. I went to have a chat with my friend Archbishop Art Brown. I recalled that when the Telegram tried a Sunday paper, some of the church organized against it and ministers blasted the paper from the pulpits. The Tely replied by putting boxes in front of the church. That didn't work and neither did the paper. The bank pulled the plug several months later.

Listen To This Guy

"The easiest thing is to get the idea; the hardest thing is to implement it; but the things that create risk can also guarantee our future." That was me announcing the start of a Sunday paper, the *Sunday Sun*.

Six months later it represented forty percent of our total revenue in Toronto. A year later, practically every establishment newspaper in the country was planning to publish on Sunday.

At that time, an open Sabbath was not on. It wasn't nearly as bad in 1973. I asked Art if he would form a panel to contribute a column for us every Sunday. He quickly agreed and did so. (When you think of it, though, the church's objections were symbolic since the majority of work involved in producing a Sunday paper is in fact done on Saturday. Delivery is the only thing done on Sunday.)

There were no surveys, no outside experts, no focus groups. Just our strong feelings that we were on a roll. We had a great relationship with our readers, so we decided to go for it.

Some of the board, led by Worthington, thought it was too soon, but Rudy Bratty cast the decisive GO vote. Once again, we were walking down a new street.

It turned out to be the Yellow Brick Road.

No one could compute the number of overtime hours worked, dummies dummied, assignments done, or fights fought to get ready for the *Sunday Sun* start-up. Nor could we compute the hours worked by our first editor, Phil Sykes, who at the time was fighting a losing battle with cancer.

One year, ten months and fifteen days after the first Sun, came the first *Sunday Sun*. The page one picture was of two guys who won a contest in England picking the "ugliest men in the world." These guys were cash winners. Together, they most likely made it the worst front page of our history.

I grimaced and said: "Great paper, Phil. Great page one." After all, one of two isn't bad. I didn't comment on the lead article of the inside section which was headed: "Everything You Ever Wanted to Know About Sex — They Dared to Find Out."

Phil wanted discreet Sunshine Girls, no Rimstead, no Sunday editorials, and a couple of other things which made me cringe. But I wasn't going to argue with him. Without him we wouldn't be standing there taking bows.

Don Hunt put it best: "There has never been a newspaper that began publishing a Sunday newspaper with a zero home delivery base and went to a circulation of 65,000."

Damned if we hadn't done it again. Within a year, we were over 200,000.

After Phil died, Rimstead appeared, the girls got a little cheekier, and Worthington's editorials were once again saving the world.

But, to this day, in my mind, the paper reminds me instantly of his Herculean efforts. I'll never forget them or him. My buddy, Hartley Steward, took over the *Sunday Sun* and drove it to greater heights.

As one of the instigators of the paper, I drank a toast with Marilyn on the twentieth anniversary of the Sunday paper. We found it ironic that some of the directors who voted against it were up front taking bows. We thought it might have been nice to honour a few of the day-oners.

The Sunday paper remains the largest money-spinner. It once represented forty-five percent of our total advertising dollars.

I don't know how many English language Sunday papers there are now in Canada. I know there were none, outside of Victoria, when we started ours.

Anyway, the Sunday paper was a resounding success with everyone involved, including staff. The daily continued to be strong. The world was our oyster, so why not a rebellion?

In late April of 1974, I received a long memo from Ed Monteith, our managing editor. It signalled our first real crisis. He called it "an executive battle." What had begun as a spark of unrest in the editorial department, where these things almost always begin, had grown to an out-of- control grass fire. Uprising, too, might describe it.

It may have been centred in the editorial department, but one of the leaders was Jim Brown, the former Sun controller, who thought from the beginning I spent too much money and wasn't the right guy for the publisher's job. To be fair, I never thought much of him either.

The old Eclipse building didn't give us much room or privacy. Everyone knew each other's views — or thought they did. One of the by-products of this, inevitably, was a strain on morale.

It was very much a case of the old saw: "It ain't what a man don't know that makes him ignorant — it's what he knows that ain't so."

The affair quickly escalated to threats of dismissals. That was no rumour. I knew the instigators and I decided I should fire Joan Sutton and Andy Donato. Then I would recommend to the board that Peter Worthington be fired as editor and removed from the board.

I thought long and hard about that option. The problem was that from day one I had a small list of people "I can't do without." All three were on that list — and near the top.

I did not retreat then, nor have I retreated since, from my beliefs about spending. It was especially appropriate in the early days. We were underpaying almost everyone on staff. There was no extra pay for the long overtime hours much of the staff worked, and nearby were the Star and the Globe, paying the highest newspaper salaries in Canada.

I felt that tangible recognition of those efforts, plus a lunch or dinner with one of the top three, were important in our efforts to keep the Newspaper Guild from organizing our newspaper. So, too, were our seminars, sabbaticals and other "extravagances."

I'm sure this attitude helped bring me down in 1992, but I'm still totally convinced it was and is the right way.

In 1974, the principals out to get me seemed to be columnist Joan Sutton, cartoonist Andy Donato, production director John Webb, Worthington and Brown. But the guy in charge of plotting was Eddie Goodman, the man who had originally put together the money which gave us our start.

That gave me some consolation, because earlier Eddie had tried to get me to fire Worthington because he had written an editorial favouring the Arabs. Not much later he went after Don Hunt. Both efforts failed, but I thought it logical he should take the third strike against me.

The whole thing finally ended around the boardroom table at Goodman and Goodman. I made the point that it was a lousy time for a revolution. The paper was just beginning to make real progress. Profits, ad lineage and circulation were at their highest level ever. That being the case, why change things?

Thank God saner heads prevailed. Although Hunt thought I was crazy, I decided not to fire anyone.

Ironically, it was Sutton, Donato and Worthington who were among my greatest supporters in 1992 when coup two got me. That sort of reversal is very Sun-like and perhaps one of the reasons it works well.

I was and am most thankful they hung in with me. To be fair to Eddie Goodman, win, lose or draw he put the issue behind him and helped everyone settle down. He tells me he had nothing to do with coup two and I believe him.

While there were no dismissals, Jim Brown did take off quickly. Just ahead of my boot.

CHAPTER 10

Onward and Westward

November 1, 1971 is a significant date for most all of the original or near-original *Toronto Sun* staff. It was the start of the first competitive daily in Canada in many decades. A second important date for us was September 16, 1973, when a split board — by one vote — allowed us to begin a Sunday paper.

There are an amazing number of other significant dates in our company's brief lifetime.

On February 4, 1978, we announced we would start a daily Sun in Edmonton on April 2nd of that year. It seemed hectic at the time, but I was to learn over the years that nothing is routine about the start-up of a new daily newspaper. I remember standing near our rented press two hours after our deadline. We had yet to print one paper. I heard a muffled voice from under the press.

"Can someone get my wrench from the trunk of my car?" it said.

Someone did and, as if by magic, the press started. The staff gave me a replica of that wrench at the *Edmonton Sun*'s tenth birthday.

Edmonton didn't make money for four years. Since then

they have managed to repay the parent company, and now own their own press building and a large Metro press. (They rent office space.)

In 1980, for less than $1 million, we purchased the assets of the *Calgary Albertan* and started a daily Sun there on August 3, 1980. It also took four years to become profitable. It owns its own building, land and presses.

Don Campbell of Maclean Hunter and I had several discussions throughout all this expansion. His interest in buying the Sun stemmed from his belief that his large media company would benefit from expansion into newspapers.

My concern was different. To the best of my knowledge, few, if any, of our backers had buy/sell agreements, and someone was buying Sun shares in Montreal. (It turned out to be the CN Pension Fund, who now own fourteen percent of the Sun Corporation.)

I reported the buying to the board, and mentioned the Maclean Hunter interest. The board didn't take long to reject the idea of selling. My senior staff people also made it quite clear that they thought I was nuts to think about it. I put the matter on the agenda again a few months later. Once again, a resounding no. They also nixed my recommendation that we hedge our bets on Edmonton and do it with Maclean Hunter as a partner.

However, at yet another golf game at Lambton, some of the directors, a little leery of our western expansion, asked if I thought Don Campbell might still be interested in buying into the Sun. I said I thought so.

In fact, he was still interested, and very graciously would stick to the price he had originally offered. Our board wasn't willing to give up control just yet. An argument ensued as to the right formula by which to value the shares two or three years out. In the end we sold them fifty percent for $55 million in May of 1982. In return (and also to keep the CRTC happy), they would only put two directors on our board, plus they would enter into a standstill agreement to last five years. It meant a hands-off policy on their part. Until 1992, they honoured the agreement in full. The standstill, more simply put, meant they would vote for our state of affairs and basically not interfere.

Two years later, they made a rights offer to get them to fifty-one percent and they have continued to increase their holdings from time to time. They presently own about sixty-two percent of the Sun Corporation shares.

We learned bitterly in Edmonton that we weren't as bright as we thought we were. First of all, we hired locally, which was a mistake, and secondly, we hadn't concerned ourselves at all with the long bitter winters. On one frigid Edmonton morning alone, thirty-seven percent of our youthful delivery force quit.

Bill Bagshaw, a very popular radio man, was our choice to be publisher. We had to knock him out of the box in the very early days. I very much regret the whole Bagshaw affair.

He was (and is) a great guy — knowledgeable and popular. He knew a lot about a lot of things, but not about running newspapers — especially newspapers starting from scratch. We bit the bullet quickly and Don Hunt went to run Edmonton until we found a replacement. There is no doubt in my mind that Bill could run the up-and-going *Edmonton Sun* today. I don't mean he ever will, we've gone too far for that, but he could.

We paid attention to our Edmonton lessons in Calgary. We

purchased the old *Calgary Albertan*, which at the time was a morning business paper, from Lord Thomson, also for less than $1 million. Then we added a new press and soon our colour reproduction was as good as that of Southam's Calgary paper, the Herald.

For the Calgary launch, I formed a team of four — Les Pyette, Bob Jelenic, Tom MacMillan and Hartley Steward — to move temporarily to Calgary and supervise a plan which would be geared to separate the Sun from the Albertan. The Albertan had changed to a tabloid shortly before we purchased it. And it was most definitely a tab produced by a broadsheet staff.

Steward stayed on to be publisher and brought the *Calgary Sun* to profitability before returning to Toronto. Pyette stayed on as editor-in-chief until he, too, was needed back in Toronto.

Of course, once again everything that could go wrong did, but this time we knew how to fix it.

At the time we purchased the Albertan, John Tory, Ken Thomson's number-two man, asked if we wanted to buy the land. After some discussion, we decided to phone Gordon Gray, president of Royal LePage and also a friend of the two of us. Gray would have it appraised and we would have an opportunity to buy or decline at the price set by Gray.

The appraisal came in at $5.5 million, but was recommended against at the time because Calgary was overbuilt. For another reason as well, I said we'd take a pass. We didn't have $5.5 million. Tory put it up for sale. About a year later, it sold for $23 million. Its present worth is about $6 million.

I guess it proves you should be ready to go for the home run when the opportunity arises. However, with my total lack of expertise in the real estate field, I'd do what I did again. While the western papers were heading toward profitability at a rapid pace, back in Toronto things were booming. The 80's was our decade.

By mid-1983 the Toronto Sun Corporation was in fine shape.

We were healthy and loaded for bear. We aimed our sights south of the border.

We arrived in Houston almost by mistake. A small group of us were returning from Chicago, where the Sun Times was for sale, and we were preparing a bid on it.

As there is in any of these huge deals, there were a few big ifs. The Sun Times' owner was Marshall Fields so we hoped to make a deal which included some of his department store advertising.

Jim Hoge, a very bright young man, was the *Chicago Sun Times* publisher. He was busy scrambling for local money to make an employees' bid for ownership. Jim later went on to become publisher of the *New York Daily News*.

I felt we could overcome that difficulty. Hoge and I hit it off quite well, both being editorial guys. He told me the employees' fear was that Rupert Murdoch might buy the paper, which he later did.

We knew Murdoch was considering a bid, since I'd received a message from him pointing out it wouldn't be in anyone's interest to get into a bidding war. I agreed, but Don Hunt and I had already decided we would arrive at a price and if they didn't like it, we'd walk away.

The paper owned some prime real estate on the river where the Sun Times was printed. Unfortunately, new presses were desperately needed, and this building couldn't accommodate them.

Sun Times' circulation was steady in the centre of the city, but was declining in the suburbs; most of the losses were going to the *Chicago Tribune*. Unfortunately, the advertising money was in the suburbs. We felt we could overcome that, too.

We arranged for a board meeting and I sent the directors a fairly detailed report. Back on the plane, Don Hunt was saying that he was on-side with the thinking on the Sun Times, but felt it would be responsible of us to check into the *Houston Post* which was also for sale, at an asking price of $175 million.

There seemed to be no way we could handle that kind of money, but I agreed we should at least look at it.

Peter Eby, vice-chairman of Burns Fry, was helping us with the Chicago bid so he said he would contact the Post's agent.

The next day, he phoned to say the Post management was disdainful of tabloids and would not furnish us with any information. We decided we'd send them some more details and see if we could get a more positive reaction. We did, and the information didn't take long to arrive.

The Post management had found out painfully that there was very little interest in second papers in the U.S. — certainly not at that price and in the poor Houston economy.

Lynn Carpenter, my assistant, brought the Post information package to us as we boarded the plane. Nothing like being prepared.

We were to meet with the Post people the next day in the early morning at an unfinished Houston hotel called the Remington. They were going to look at us, but try not to admit we were potential buyers. I was the tour guide for our group since I had spent one night in Houston a few years previously when we went down to see an Oiler football game.

We dined that evening at Caruso's where the waiters and waitresses all sing. Then we decided to have a nightcap at the Remington, where we were to meet in about twelve hours.

Unfortunately, there were two Remingtons in Houston. We wanted the hotel. We got a disco in a bad part of town. When we arrived at the hotel the next morning, we were paying slightly for our hour at the disco. I was glad it would be just a quick walk-through. There was no way we were in the $175 million league.

On our look through the Post financial statements, I could see bad debts of $13 million for circulation. It stuck out like a sore thumb. Impossible, I thought. I asked for a brief recess and said to Eby and Bob Jelenic, a senior Sun financial guy: "Let's look at this a little longer, but let's not mention circulation."

We wound up offering $94 million for the Post. "I don't think Mrs. Hobby (the matriarch of the family which owned the Post) will take it," her advisor, Jim Crowther said. "She is very proud, and she has told friends she isn't taking less than $100 million."

"Well," I said weakly, "you could tell her that $94 million U.S. is about equal to $100 million Canadian." Jim did and, to my surprise, they accepted our offer.

Then we took our run at the circulation. It had been announced publicly and in their prospectus as being as large as 395,000 daily. We thought it was maybe 340,000 to 350,000. It turned out to be more like 315,000 or even a bit less.

Jelenic and I took Harry Hayes, the general manager, to lunch and confronted him with our view of circulation. Harry argued and hedged and finally cried, and admitted that the circulation was "about 350,000." Amazingly, he had recovered in a couple of hours when Mrs. Hobby called her last meeting of the Post executive committee.

"What's the circulation Harry?" Mrs. Hobby asked. "Well Ma'am," Harry said, "it's nice to announce a new record for the daily at just over 400,000 last week."

No wonder there is no deep water within fifty miles of Houston. Harry, abetted by the Chronicle, has likely dried up the river bed throwing papers into it every night.

I was busy teaching Eby how to work on circulation in this manner. We were preparing for his confrontation with the Post's representatives who didn't seem to know anything about circulation either.

"How much do you think we should get off the bill?" Peter asked. I thought if we got a discount of between $1 million and $2 million, we would be delighted. Anything over that would be gravy.

Peter spent the day in New York negotiating. He phoned two or three times with nothing to say other than to report that his opponent was seeking direction from Houston. "How would $6 million off sound to you?" Eby finally asked. I could have kissed him. We had acquired the *Houston Post*, one of American's major dailies, for $88 million.

Later we were having a beer while we waited for the lawyers to say we could sign. Don was asking Peter how his fee was determined. Eby told him it amounted to about one percent of the total amount of the sale.

I was on holidays when Eby's bill for $94,000 arrived. Don changed it to $88,000, thus penalizing Eby $6,000 for the $6 million he had saved us with his negotiations. I was furious. We straightened that out in a hurry.

The next day, Mrs. Hobby, a very classy lady, led her family into the cafeteria. I was walking behind her, watching the expressions on the faces of the family and staff.

The *New York Times* had had people in town the day before, and most of them thought they were being taken over by the Times.

After a very emotional speech, Mrs. Hobby introduced me.

"Who is this red-haired guy with manure on his boots? Surely he couldn't have bought our paper." I could read it on their faces.

I hastened to assure them that there would be no big housecleaning, and that the Post would certainly remain broadsheet.

Unknown to me, at the same time in Toronto, Worthington was giving an exclusive interview to our new competition — the *Houston Chronicle*. "Don't believe Creighton," he told their reporter. "He'll turn it tab in no time with a page three Sunshine Girl."

So began our Texas odyssey.

I remember looking at the first issue of the *Houston Post* preserved in the library. It read like news from the recent past ... the Russians were threatening Afghanistan ... Houston was being described as "murder city"... the Democrats and Republicans were holding a state-wide election and, on the top of the first column on page one, was a little story saying: "Newspaper for Sale ... business good, desire to change is the only reason for selling."

It was still some newspaper, even though it was failing.

O. Henry had worked there. William P. Hobby had worked in the circulation department in 1885. He had bought the Post in 1939 when he was governor of Texas. After his death, his widow, Oveta Culp Hobby, became its chairman. In 1942, she became Colonel Hobby and formed the Women's Army Corp., known throughout the world as the WACs.

In the 40's she appeared on the cover of *Time* magazine. Later, she became the second woman to hold a cabinet post in the U.S. government. She was in charge of health, education, and welfare for Eisenhower.

If you landed in Houston, it was at Hobby Airport. If you visited Rice University, you saw many tributes to the Hobby family. And the newspaper plant, a state of the art facility, was known throughout the city as Fort Hobby. From it, they publish seven days a week, 365 days a year.

Its land, building, new colour presses, and computers were valued at more than $80 million. We owned four different buildings sitting on seventeen acres near the Galleria area of Houston which is a prime location.

The Post had 1,840 full-time employees (only 484 were unionized). It was with passing interest that I learned upon going through their budget, that the year before we bought it the Post spent more on postage and long distance calls than the total amount of money we raised initially to start the *Toronto Sun*.

Back in 1982, *Houston Post* employees telephoned 12,000 people a day and visited 5,000 people door-to-door in order to pick up 1,000 new subscribers. That translated into over 100,000 calls per week and $5.3 million per year. They ran through every name in the telephone book four times a year.

Houston, at the time of our purchase was the fourth largest city in the nation. Only New York, Los Angeles and Chicago were larger.

The Post's competitor, the Chronicle, had been published since the turn of the century and had been owned by a private foundation, Houston Endowment Inc. since 1956. We knew that provisions of the Tax Reform Act of 1969 compelled the foundation to dispose of not less than fifty percent of its stock ownership by May 1989. They solved this by selling to Hearst for a mind-boggling $415 million. I hope they got a piece of the Yellow Brick Road thrown in.

The net paid circulation claimed by the Chronicle was 438,760. The Saturday and Sunday circulations were 432,112 and 528,831 with market shares of 50 percent and 53.7 percent respectively. We didn't believe it.

Total advertising lines claimed by the Chronicle was 111,235,000. We did believe that.

The product at the time was very similar to the Post which was grey, lacked local pictures, didn't run enough colour and should have had more local columnists.

Peter O'Sullivan, who we moved from the editor's job at the *Toronto Sun*, thought the Post staff was young, ambitious and eager for change. Generally, staff morale was good.

We did nothing as dramatic as changing the paper to tabloid, but we did make improvements. We implemented a daily features index, a new masthead, a new typeface, and a daily feature on the front page that was accompanied by colour art work.

We limited the number of turns on the front page, making it easier to read. We took the ads off page three and made it clear for news. We gave the editorial page and the opinion pages a section of their own, thus giving far more prominence to the comment and opinion part of the paper. This also allowed for a colour cartoon. We appointed the paper's major and most popular columnist, Lynn Ashby, as editor. He was a good choice.

Our readers certainly knew we had arrived.

For many years, the Post operated out of cramped downtown quarters on St. Charles Street. In 1981, they moved their offices and built an offset printing plant on the Southwest Freeway near the famous Galleria Shopping Centre.

The offset plant contained twenty-six units of Goss Metro presses — not enough to print the entire run of the Post. So the run was split between the modern plant and the old letterpress plant which contained forty-one out-dated press units with no real colour capacity. We rented this premise for one year with an option to renew for six months. Then we took the seven Metro units originally planned for Calgary and installed them in the Houston presshall.

The presses were shipped from England. About half-way across the Atlantic, the ship ran into a fierce storm. One of the units went overboard. We managed to get another with minimum delay. Maybe it was an omen that things wouldn't be all sweetness and light.

The Hobby family were to leave when the deal was signed. It must have been traumatic for Mrs. Hobby. I don't think she ever returned to the Post.

We also arranged as part of the deal for the executive director, vice-president of sales and marketing, and the managing editor to depart when the purchase was completed.

Don Hunt became the general manager. I was the publisher. Peter O'Sullivan stayed as editor-in-chief. Marvin Naftolin, the *Toronto Sun*'s director of advertising, also moved to Houston to run the Post's advertising.

So far, so good. We'd saved a few bodies and a few salaries.

Getting to know Texas and the Texans was a delight.There

was millionaire Stanley Marsh III who had a sign at the entrance of his posh farm which read: "Future home of the world's largest poisonous snake farm." At a party he threw for a visiting Japanese trade delegation, the only guests invited were Texans at least six feet, four inches tall.

There was Baron Enrico Portanova, born in Texas incidentally, who air-conditioned the entire backyard of his mother-in-law's Houston home because his wife said: "We like good weather."

His first wife was a beautiful former member of the Yugoslavian national women's basketball team. They were evicted from their first apartment when the neighbours complained that his wife kept them awake by dribbling basketballs on the living room floor in the middle of the night. Their monkey was also a problem.

The Baron's second wife was Sandy Hooas of Lamar, Texas. Soon after the marriage, Sandy became Sandra ... then Sondra ... then Alessandra ... and now, Baroness Alessandra.

In 1980, the *New York Times* reported that the Baron was buying the 21 Club in New York (one of my favourite restaurants) as a birthday present for his Baroness. The deal didn't go through.

Then there was Eddy Chiles, the owner of the Texas Rangers, who took out full-page ads advising the government what to do. He was brief. "Defend our shores, deliver our mail and leave us the hell alone."

Billy Bob's Bar in Fort Worth had phone booths that made it easier to lie to your boss or wife. Each booth had a selection of piped-in background sounds. "Hi dear, I'm still at the office," could be spoken to the sounds of keyboard clacking and phones ringing. "Just leaving the airport, sir," could be accompanied by the sounds of jet planes overhead.

The serious discussion over our future with the *Houston Post* began during a golf game with Herb Solway. I said that while we were profitable, the Houston economy was still terrible and we had lots of money at risk if our share of advertising went down. I knew there were expansion opportunities in Canada, but wouldn't recommend any of them to the board until the question mark about Houston was removed.

Solway asked if we could find anyone to buy the Post. Off the top of my head, I said Robert Maxwell. Failing that, I said we'd have to find a rich Texan with an ego.

Maxwell never got beyond the stage of saying he was interested, but we found our Texan. His name was Dean Singleton. Besides filling our criteria he was, bless him, a journalist.

Negotiations were hot and heavy, but we finally made a deal. We settled for $150 million cash, but also would get a share of any increased advertising lineage. Dean did his deal with the banks. All we had to do was wait for the closing date which was October 20th. Unfortunately, our world crashed on October 19, 1987.

Who knows how many deals fell apart during that period as the financial world panicked? Thanks mainly to Eby and Singleton, whose bank arrangements held firm, we kept our deal together.

We got $100 million cash, with $50 million to come. There is still a real question mark about that $50 million, but I think the Sun will get it eventually. Remember the Texas ego.

Unlike a lot of Canadian businesses which lost their Texas boots during those rough days, we made minimum profits, even discounting the $50 million still owed.

We originally paid $88 million and spent $15 million on more presses and related equipment. In the years we held it, we made about $20 million in operating profit, so we could certainly hold our heads up.

Now we were in a position to expand further. Nonetheless, it was the first time we'd deserted a product that we'd bought or started. I didn't like the feeling.

Marilyn and I stayed in a rented apartment in Houston, going back and forth to Canada, for about nine months. It wasn't like Toronto. Firstly, and surprising to us, shopping was better in Houston. There weren't too many people in them, but the major stores in Houston were all within a mile of each other. Marilyn had a car and the interest, so it was a scary combination.

Almost as scary was the crime in Houston. We never

Did She Get It At Saks?

Marilyn Creighton returning from Houston, Texas after the Sun purchased the *Houston Post*, was asked by the customs officer: "Did you buy anything while you were away?"

"Just a newspaper," Marilyn replied.

had anything happen to us, but it took a while to get used to the fortress-like mentality of the city.

The Post, for instance, was spending $1 million on both internal and external security forces. To a Canadian, it was mind-boggling. We set out to change it. Fortunately for me,

Don Hunt was in charge of security after both of us met the head of the outside protective group.

We asked: "Where can we cut?" His answer was simple: "Nowhere." He told Don and me that the week before we took over, security had found a naked lady in the parking lot. She'd escaped a car on the thruway, but not before she'd been robbed and ravished.

Don was later able to cut costs in a strange way. It was discovered that several of our internal police force were pushing drugs inside the Post, and they were let go.

About eight months into our Houston adventure, we experienced a series of typical Houston mini-dramas that helped us decide to return to Toronto more quickly than we had planned.

It began on a day I burned the bottom of my feet on the cement flooring around the pool at 7:30 a.m. That evening we went to see Placido Domingo. We had reserved parking inside and were met on the floor by a large off-duty policeman with one of the biggest revolvers I've ever seen.

The next day I was driving with Marilyn in the car when suddenly dozens of policemen arrived on the scene and blocked all traffic for the arrival of vice-president George Bush, who owned a condominium in our building.

Doug Sanders, one of my favourite golf professionals, had invited me to play nine holes with George Bush just after Marilyn and I had moved in. The vice-president, I thought, was a down-to-earth good guy. But the security inflicted on him made me feel like I was in the charge of the Light Brigade.

It was shortly after a number of these security incidents that Marilyn and I returned to Toronto on a long-weekend pass to see, you guessed it, Placido Domingo, who this time was singing at the O'Keefe Centre and who would sing afterwards at the home of Elvio and Marlene Del Zotto.

We had a wonderful day which began with a beer on the patio of the Encore restaurant before the performance. It seemed we knew and were greeted by everyone who came by. Domingo was in great form at the theatre and Elvio persuaded him to sing "Happy Birthday" to Marilyn. She melted.

"That's enough for us," we thought. "We're coming back home." I didn't have much time legally left to stay in the States, anyway.

Travel is grand; home is better.

John McDermott

Of all the success stories at the Sun, one that pleased me most was John McDermott, who has a golden voice to go with his temperament. John now has a best-selling recording. It's wonderful listening, and I'm sure will be played again and again.

John, who has held a few positions at the Sun, was nice enough to thank me (and others) on the cover notes to his album. This might be taken to mean that I'd given him money, as others did.

Actually, I taught him to sing!

CHAPTER 11

Legal Beagles

A few of my friends thought I should have been a lawyer. I don't know about that, but I certainly enjoy being with lawyers.

I loved covering the courts. It was a sheer joy to listen to the greats like John Robinette or Arthur Martin or Charlie Dubin pontificating on the law. I loved, too, the intensity and humanity of Arthur Maloney.

The chief justice when I was in the courts was Bill Gale. The first time he ever saw me was when I fell asleep in his court. I've never been awakened by a chief justice since.

After the Sun started, about the only way for me to get to court again was to be summoned (or arrested, I guess).

I was summoned once when John Munro, then a Liberal cabinet minister, successfully sued the Sun. While I had no real connection with the story, I was giving evidence as the publisher of the paper. It lasted for two days, and it was very painful because we hadn't handled the story well at all.

Mr. Justice John Holland assessed the Sun for the largest libel settlement up until then in Canadian courts. The only joy I got was his description of me as "candid." He said I was "helpful, articulate and knowledgeable. One of the best witnesses I've heard."

Those sentences were sent to me circled, with a red arrow pointing to the margin. Scribbled there was a note from my lawyer, Cliff Lax. "And the stupidest," he had written.

Another time, charges were levelled against the Sun, Peter Worthington and me under the Official Secrets Act. Upon conviction, we could have been liable for a mandatory fourteen-year jail sentence.

Marilyn and I were at the airport with our son Donald. We were on our way to Los Angeles to tour a couple of movie studios. An Air Canada employee came to us and asked if we would please go to the first class lounge. I thought this was very nice of the airline.

When we reached the lounge, however, someone handed me a phone, and when I took it an unfamiliar voice said I would be able to hear a statement being read in the House regarding the Sun and the Official Secrets Act. "Stay on the line when the statement is over."

Incredulously I listened. At one point it sounded like we had committed treason. It was an RCMP guy on the phone and he suggested that I wait in the lounge for an hour so that they could come there and officially charge me. I said the plane was leaving in fifteen minutes, and talked them into doing it in Edmonton on my way home.

The charges revolved around a column by Worthington revealing Soviet activity in Canada. The material used was clearly marked "secret." Worthington's position was a) if you send documents to sixty-seven people, which they did, then it's no longer secret, and b) it was all old hat anyway.

My view was the same as Worthington's except that our

lawyer had said it was a dangerous story to run. On that basis I had told Worthington not to run it. He went with it anyway.

My lawyer was John Robinette. I suspected these charges were politically inspired and I knew John favoured the Grits. But on this one he was a friend looking after a friend. His bill was the cheapest of the four lawyers.

Eddie Goodman and David Stockwood represented the Sun and Julian Porter represented Worthington. Peter and I needed separate counsel because he might have ended up in an adversarial position.

After months of sitting in the prisoner's box, which was very demeaning, Judge Carl Waisberg became my new very best friend by throwing out the charges without Peter or me testifying. He agreed, in part at least, with Worthington.

Outside the court at a press conference, Peter was having a ball. I had one lonely reporter next to me. "I wonder what Worthington's saying," the reporter said.

"I think he wants to appeal," I said.

◆ ◆ ◆

If I enjoyed lawyers, I was crazy about judges. And their dogs. Especially their dogs.

I took an automatic liking to Supreme Court Judge Campbell Grant's dog, Baron. Campbell had a cottage two doors from us in Port Elgin, Ontario.

The *Toronto Sun*'s editor, John Downing, a former Telegram reporter and editor and a rather pontifical fellow, was using our cottage for a week. He was sitting on the sand reading a book when the judge and Baron appeared on their morning beach walk.

As is his custom, John launched into a tirade about whatever his latest cause was. Mr. Justice Grant listened impatiently, but not as impatiently as Baron. He had a job to do. Showing ultimate dog sense and impeccable timing, he walked purposefully towards Downing and piddled on his leg. In one minute Baron became my favourite dog.

I ran into Baron several times afterwards, but didn't actually speak to him until the late 80's.

Jim McCallum, my lawyer and former Sun board member, called to ask if I'd seen Campbell Grant lately. I hadn't seen the judge for about a year, but I knew that despite his age he remained active. His lovely wife Grace had passed away and Campbell had retired from the bench, although he heard the odd case as a supernumerary judge.

McCallum asked if I would contact Campbell to see if he was still healthy enough to handle a case. I did and he was. We had a pleasant chat and I prepared to ring off. "You can't go until you talk to Baron," Campbell said. "Of course not," I said. After a brief silence I heard a bark on the other end of the phone. "Good evening to you Baron, have you run into John Downing lately?" Another bark.

"He wants you to give Marilyn our best," the judge said.

I phoned McCallum. "Campbell can handle a case easily," I assured him. "But be sure to stay on the right side of Baron."

Shopping Spree

On November 20, 1987, we sold the *Houston Post* for $150 million U.S. We had paid $88 million U.S. for it in December 1983.

Audit Bureau of Circulation figures for 1987 showed the *Toronto Sun* daily at 302,000. We had registered the highest annual jump in circulation in Canada. Our six-month gain was 12,600 papers. In the number-two position was the *Vancouver Sun* with a gain of 4,300. The *Calgary Sun* was in fourth place with a gain of 3,500 in a six-month period.

On Sunday, *Montreal La Presse*, with a gain of 9,900 papers, edged out the *Calgary Sun* at plus 9,500 and the *Toronto Sun* at plus 8,800. The *Edmonton Sun* was a quite respectable plus 7,000 for fifth place.

The *Toronto Sun*, our cash cow, showed revenues in April 1987 of $12.2 million, twenty percent ahead of 1986, for the best single period in the history of the company.

We now had extra cash, and we had finished our experiment in Texas on a lot better footing than most Canadian investors in the Lone Star state had.

The money was burning a hole in our pockets. We bought the weekly *Financial Post* division from our parent company, Maclean Hunter, for $46.8 million. Then we sold twenty-five percent of it to Pearson plc., publishers of the *Financial Times* in London, England for $11.5 million, and another fifteen percent to Conrad Black's Hollinger Inc. for $6.9 million. We retained sixty percent. I was delighted.

Not only had we hedged our bets but we had two partners who would contribute greatly to the product.

Taking the weekly *Financial Post* daily was likely the Sun's biggest roll of the dice. For eighteen years on and off, Maclean Hunter had been looking at the viability of turning their weekend product into a daily and publishing it six days a week.

Another voice — and one which impressed me more than the Maclean Hunter voices — was that of my friend, Conrad Black. Conrad had for years been aching to go head to head with the Globe and its *Report on Business*.

He was sure that he could involve the *Financial Times of London* both as a partner and as a provider of their complete news wire, which I believe is the best source of financial news in the world.

Conrad was exciting and excited. He also wanted part of the action. With him and the *Financial Times* interested, how could we resist? Conrad had some figures to prove it was a viable venture, but I suspect he was interested mainly because of the Globe's ROB. Maybe even more important, he intensely disliked Globe publisher Roy Megarry, who has since retired.

Conrad had tried to buy the Globe several years before. During the bidding war, Megarry jumped onto a desk in the Globe's newsroom and spoke eloquently on the subject of why the Globe should never be sold to Black. Fortunately for him, it wasn't.

Conrad retired from that battle and went on to buy into the *Daily Telegraph* in London from which all his blessings flow.

I felt, and I'm sure I'm correct since I've seen it happen five times, that we would have to spend more than is usually needed on the *Financial Post* editorial product so as to make us the first business paper read over the ROB. The ROB, of course, would spend more than normal to fight us off.

The end result, of course, would be that both newspapers' bottom lines would be adversely affected. The big beneficiary would be, as always in these newspaper wars, the readers. Competition is a marvellous thing.

Frank Barlow, then chief executive of the *Financial Times*, was happy to take twenty-five percent of the Post, the maximum investment allowed by a foreigner in Canadian media. Conrad wanted as much as we wanted to give him. The board

Fire Burns Editor

One day at lunch Conrad Black showed me a memo from the files of the *Daily Telegraph* that someone sent him during his brilliant acquisition of that paper.

The paper's drama critic critiqued a London West End play. He wrote that he could not comment on the ending "because the theatre burned down during Act three."

The editor wrote him a gentle note the next day suggesting that if such a thing happened again, he might perhaps think of notifying the news editor and writing a brief report on the calamity.

"My Dear Editor," the critic replied. "You seem to be under a misapprehension as to the nature of my appointment with the Telegraph. I am your drama critic, not a muckraker."

thought ten percent. I said it was his idea and that he had delivered the *Financial Times* to the deal. He wound up at fifteen percent. He would have taken more but he was gracious about it and accepted our offer. For tax reasons, the *Financial Times* and Conrad now both own nineteen percent and the Sun's holdings are sixty-one percent.

I find peoples' perceptions of Conrad both amusing and confusing. A lot of people, including a few on the Sun board, have conflicting views, but I like the guy and I trust him.

I feel Conrad has been very good for the cause of journalism. He and I controlled the wire service, United Press Canada, for a few years, which certainly woke up Canadian Press. Once again, competition proved an advantage to the clients of both wire services.

Conrad and I closed the UPC deal at his house the night Bud McDougall, the head of Argus, drowned at his winter residence in Lyford Cay.

While I waited, Conrad talked to Bud's relatives and other board members. By the time he got to me, he was elated and elected to head Argus Corp.

We went to his dining room, which was large. A Spanish gentleman presented us with a seven or eight pound roast chicken. Conrad nodded to the houseman, who took the chicken to the other end of the table, and Conrad walked down to carve.

"White meat or dark?" he shouted.

"White for me," I yelled back from the other end of the room. Conrad's first slash at the chicken sliced into his hand. It bled profusely and the Spanish houseman was pulled into service as a doctor.

I sliced the chicken.

When Conrad returned, we munched on the bird. It struck me at the time that only in this business would a medium-sized newspaper publisher get the opportunity to witness the takeover of a big company and buy a wire service, all the while eating the chairman's chicken and trying to avoid the blood-stained bits.

The weekly edition of the *Financial Post* started in 1907. For eighty years many of its readers got the paper by mail. That meant that in outlying areas delivery was on Monday or Tuesday, and sometimes as late as Wednesday. Friday's stock prices were of little use the following Tuesday.

There was no home delivery at the time of our purchase, but there we were, forging ahead with big home delivery circulation projections like we knew what we were doing.

On opening night, we had a splashy black-tie dinner on the executive floor of the Sun. Afterwards, our advertisers and board members went to catch the press run. Outside the building, a winter storm was waiting in readiness to screw up the opening night circulation. It did.

In the first month, eighty-five percent of our delivery people left, along with one-third of our wholesalers.

Enter Bruce, son of president Creighton. He came from out of the bullpen in Calgary with no warm-up, but in time, he fixed it. Bruce never really wanted to work for the Sun. Nor was I anxious that he did. But when he graduated from the University of Western Ontario, thousands of people were looking for jobs.

I persuaded him to come and join our corporation out west, where I didn't go too often. He joined the *Edmonton Sun* and, soon became their leading advertising salesman. He did the same thing when he went to the *Calgary Sun*.

Bruce was transferred from Calgary to Toronto, where he finally wound up in circulation, a new game for him. One problem good circulation people have is they can never get out of the circulation department. The really good ones are so few that no one wants to lose them.

Bruce's contribution as director of circulation in Toronto was to get the daily up to 300,000. The price and the competition have both increased since then, and the daily now hovers around 250,000.

Bruce's performance won him a bid from Calgary to return as general manager. He did and liked it.

With the disastrous circulation opening of the *Financial Post Daily*, Bruce got the call from Toronto, as Les Pyette likes to say, "to come and save our ass."

The chips were on the line and Bruce reluctantly agreed. It was a long, difficult process to climb from a hole that deep, but he succeeded.

The Post has been a tough, expensive haul. But in my view it is here to stay, even in this economy.

In July of 1988, we bought Comprint, a commercial printer in Gaithersburg, Maryland, for $12.9 million. So far it's been a bit of a disappointment, but the company is improving, and it has the capacity to print a daily paper in Washington if my successor turns out to have the interest I had.

And finally, in the fall of 1988, we bought the *Ottawa Sunday Herald* for $750,000, and started a daily four months later.

But at the Sun Corporation, despite expansion, the *Toronto Sun* was always the key. It produced more than fifty percent of total revenue and a corresponding contribution to the bottom line. Its revenues for 1987 were $143 million.

In 1988, Toronto revenues jumped to $149 million and, in

1989, another record of $156 million. In 1990, we saw tangible evidence of the economy slowing down. The Toronto paper hung in, as well as some other newspapers in Canada, although revenues sputtered and dropped to $148 million.

By 1991, our gravy train started to run out of steam. Revenues dropped over $5 million to $143 million. We put the heat on expenses and saved money, but that couldn't make up for the revenue loss.

I felt obliged to write the following in my report to the shareholders:

1990 was our worst and most frustrating year. Some of the reasons were:
• Unending recession news fuelled in part by our own industry
• Impending GST
• Increased unemployment
• Higher energy and newsprint prices
All these combined to keep the consumer at home with a corresponding drop in advertising.
The main frustrations were:
• We improved our share of market in every market we competed in but in most instances the market shrank.
• In all of our divisions, our expenses were under budget and in some they were even less than the year before. Unfortunately, the drop in revenues was so graphic that savings could not replace them on the bottom line.

As well at the time we had two start-ups (the *Financial Post Daily* and the *Ottawa Sun*) on the go. It promised to be interesting.

◆ ◆ ◆

During my years at the Sun, I sadly proved that one should stick to one's day job. At various times I bought restaurants and horses and, although I had some fun, I lost more money than I had fun.

I saved a Dan Jenkins' *Sports Illustrated* column from a few years back in which he said that baseball is a game that used to be played by Babe Ruth and Ty Cobb and then by Joe DiMaggio and Ted Williams and then by Mickey Mantle and Willie Mays.

"Now," he wrote, "it's played by a bunch of guys in leotards and helmets cavorting on wall-to-wall carpet. In between innings, Tommy Lasorda discusses pasta, milkshakes and how he lost weight."

While I knew where he was coming from, I didn't agree with him. I think a lot of today's stars would have been stars in the old days.

All this is by way of background, to try to explain why the Sun invested $5 million to help buy some of that wall-to-wall carpet protected by a retractable dome.

Our main reason for taking the SkyDome plunge was simple. If it was good for Toronto, it would be good for the Sun. So we joined the Dome Consortium and in return we bought the rights to the tours of the Dome, which is a money-maker, but which more importantly, identifies us clearly with the SkyDome and the Jays.

We also have the exclusive rights to advertise in the Dome — shutting out both the Star and the Globe. Some politicians seemed to think this would give us and the other partners an opportunity to turn huge profits.

I suspect only one or two of the investors are making any money and in neither case would it be a sufficient return on their investment. I told our board that I favoured the investment, but we were investing in public relations and not to hold their breath waiting for money back.

There has been a second call for money from the original partners. We (and a few others) said we would not be making further investments.

Like my other two investments in restaurants, the Founder's Club at the SkyDome has floundered since day one. The partners contributed big bucks to get rid of its original debt, but are unlikely to be as accommodating if the call comes again.

I think the Founder's Club is an excellent restaurant set in nice surroundings. In their initial cash flow projections, the founders forecast lots of business on the nights of Blue Jays games. They were wrong. Firstly, those who use the Founder's Club don't like eating early to accommodate the ball game. Secondly, I believe people at a ball game prefer hot dogs and beer. I'm with them.

The Sun made another important investment when Bowes Publishers came to us and asked to be purchased. It began with a call to Ron Osborne of Maclean Hunter from Jim Bowes, owner, president and founder of the company.

Jim Bowes was feeling "mortal." He wasn't getting any younger (I know the feeling) and he was going through a series of debilitating tests to determine if he had cancer. He was trying to get his empire under the wing of a benevolent dictator. He had been reading and listening to the details of the standstill agreement between the Sun and Maclean Hunter. Osborne gave him my phone number.

To my shame, I had barely heard of Bowes at the time. I

knew that they had a few weeklies surrounding Edmonton and therefore were a competitor for advertising with the *Edmonton Sun*. The up side was that the Bowes group of publications supplied a pool of employees, all looking to work for a daily. *The Edmonton Sun* treated them like they were a farm team.

Bruce Jackson and I climbed on a plane for Edmonton the next day. If this group was for sale, I wanted to be there before Conrad, Thomson or Southam. Southam especially could have put together a strong advertising package by adding the Bowes weeklies to their dailies. This would have hurt our Edmonton and Calgary papers.

Bowes at that time owned small dailies in Grande Prairie and Fort McMurray, Alberta; Portage La Prairie, Manitoba; and Kenora, Ontario — four in all.

When they told us "small", they meant it. The circulation of the four dailies was only 25,000 in total. (Since then, they have added a fifth daily in St. Thomas, Ontario.)

In addition, Bowes published twenty-four weeklies and shopping guides. Shopping flyers distributed amounted to 73,000 and the weeklies to 136,000.

The company had three magazines, the *Dairy Farmer*, the *Hog Farmer* and *London Business* — a monthly magazine. Bowes also had commercial printing plants in London, Ontario; Leduc, Alberta; and Penticton, British Columbia. The monthlies had a circulation of 33,000.

In May of 1988, we paid $25 million for sixty percent of Bowes Publishers. By the end of 1991, we owned 100 percent. During those years, Bowes purchased eight more papers for $12 million. That gave us four small dailies, thirty-one weekly newspapers and shopping guides, four quar-

terly and monthly magazines, plus three commercial printing plants. A five-star purchase if there ever was one.

The deal was done without an argument, the easiest deal I
did at the Sun. We quickly got 100 percent, as mentioned,
and to make it all happily complete, Jim Bowes, who had
been ailing during negotiations, regained his health.

Bill Dempsey is now president of Bowes. Jim and his
number-two man Ken Kirkpatrick both retired after the purchase was completed. Bill had his work cut out stepping into
Jim's shoes. There was a love/respect relationship between
Jim and his employees which was great to see. Needless to
say, Jim's background was editorial.

When our deal was done, Jim used a large number of his
own shares to reward his originals and key employees.

When we purchased the company, it had no secretaries and
still doesn't. They owned only two fax machines, but visited
their properties in a private jet. When we got rid of the plane,
Jim helped sponsor the pilot in his new job.

I wasn't worried one bit about Bowes' morale, but I
thought we should make a couple of circuits around the
papers to prove we weren't ogres. It was important we kept
people happy.

I took a couple of minutes at the first annual publishers'
dinner to welcome the Bowes people to our family.

"I can only ask you to believe that you've joined a company which is at the peak of success. We are a company with
good profits and employees who are deeply loyal. We have
the goodwill of most of our companies, the admiration of our
competitors and the appreciation of our shareholders."

As the recession deepened, I would regret some of those
words.

◆ ◆ ◆

In Ottawa, I thought Marc Charlebois and Ken Lehmann an odd couple for the newspaper business. Charlebois was a former play-by-play announcer for the CFL. Ken was a wonderful player for the Ottawa Roughriders, getting two Schenley nominations and winning one, in the days when the CFL was worth watching.

They watched the success of the *Toronto Sunday Sun* and the continued reluctance of the *Ottawa Citizen* not to start a Sunday product.

Charlebois and Lehmann decided to take the plunge. The money part was simple — they mortgaged their homes. They rented office space that could charitably be called a dump, into which they managed to put two classy offices for themselves. They hired a raw, young staff who worked for very little.

They visited us asking if we would become partners. The idea appealed to me, I guess because the quarters reminded me of the Eclipse building. But I said no.

However, they did attract a few local investors and more advertising than they were really entitled to. They hit every business friend they could find and Lehmann was one tenacious ad salesman.

In addition, the circulation announced by both of them was almost always noticeably greater than the number of papers printed. That came back to haunt us for a while when we finally took over.

Our salesman would tell a prospective advertiser that the paper's circulation was at 37,000 and climbing. The odd client would pull out a note from Charlebois claiming that the circulation was 53,000 — a year earlier. "You're losing circulations," he'd say.

Painfully, we finally put that behind us.

Charlebois and Lehmann held on for five years, but the paper, starved for money, was slowly going downhill.

Marc kept approaching the Sun Corporation and we kept saying no. But the way the real circulation hung in with the fledging Herald impressed me. Also, the people we sent there to scout it out all came back feeling it was worth a try.

In August of 1988, while the *Toronto Sun* was churning out more money than ever before, we purchased the assets of the Herald for under $1 million. Three weeks later, an *Ottawa Sunday Sun* was born.

Almost immediately the *Ottawa Citizen* responded. We were expecting this, but not as quickly nor in such an aggressive manner. They gave their new Sunday paper away free to their subscribers. Two months later, on November 7, 1988, the *Ottawa Sun* went daily, and another battle with Southam had begun.

The critics said Ottawa was not a Sun-type city. Obviously we thought they were wrong and invested heartily in our beliefs. We brought in some senior editorial people from Toronto, rented vastly improved space, and bought a new Urbanite press and a building to house it.

My youngest son, Donald, I'm proud to say, was part of the Ottawa startup. He's still with them as director of marketing. His publisher calls him "a very valuable guy."

So far, the results have been very much in our favour.

In the first year Sunday circulation increased by thirty-three percent to 37,000. Ad lineage increased by eighteen percent, giving us nineteen percent of market share compared to thirteen percent when we took over.

As the recession continues, the increases are slower, but

with daily circulation at more than 50,000 and Sunday around 70,000 and still rising, the *Ottawa Sun* people are extremely confident.

The harder the conflict, the more glorious the triumph.

Hartley Steward and his staff have, so far, provided us with our best start ever.

◆ ◆ ◆

"What's the most we can pay for your papers?" growled Peter Eby from the shadow of our couch on the patio of our Florida condominium. Peter and I were in our bathing suits having just come up from a morning swim. In front of us, sweating from the heat and wearing a black pin-striped suit, stood John Mayo, head of a group of Florida-based weekly papers and shoppers, which we ended up purchasing from our English partners, Pearson plc.

We paid them $18.3 million for the group, which was profitable when we purchased it in 1989. Soon after, the Florida economy began to stutter. Now it is worse. Eby and I are beginning to think his opening line, which might have been a good one at the time, is wearing as thin as the Florida economy.

In 1990, under the leadership of Peter O'Sullivan, the company produced a colourful weekly (called *The Weekly*) and began marketing it in the Orlando area. If it succeeded, the plan was to gradually market it state-wide.

Peter is a veteran Sun editor, having run both the *Toronto Sun* and the *Houston Post* news rooms. He left Houston when we sold it to Dean Singleton and he landed in St. Louis where Ralph Ingersol started the *St. Louis Sun* in competition with the Pulitzer paper — the *Post Dispatch*.

There was a lot of publicity when the time arrived to publish and there was nothing wrong with the content of the new paper. Mr. Ingersol's pockets just weren't deep enough to hang on long enough to really find out if the *St. Louis Sun* would work.

We'd been offered a piece of the St. Louis paper and happily for us had declined. As we moved O'Sullivan into Florida to put out *The Weekly*, we decided that that would be the end of our shopping spree for the moment.

CHAPTER 13

See The World ...

My mother died of cancer at age fifty-two. She was one of my best friends. In her era, you paid your own medical bills. My dad was given early retirement when a British firm took over Boxer Wallpaper, where he'd worked for over thirty years. The day after he retired, the company came to take his car. He had to buy it and that put his bank account about as close as you'd want to zero.

Sometime before, he had had to turn his insurance policies into cash and, just before mom died, he had to pawn her engagement ring. He was forced to move into our place, on a pension of just under twenty dollars a month. He tried very hard to sell real estate or to get a sales job. It was a tough time, although the old age pension helped. Finally cancer hit him in the mouth. Death was slow, embarrassing and painful. He died at seventy-two.

To the end he was a great friend. It was so sad.

Marilyn has parents with great longevity. Her dad was ninety-four when he died as I was writing this book. Her mother is ninety-two and is in a nursing home. She is a tough, excellent mother. Our kids and their kids visit her and write her regularly. There is a wonderful bond between them.

My mother and father really never travelled except occasionally, due to my dad's job. The Chamberlains, Marilyn's parents, moved to England after her father retired from his own leather goods shop at sixty-five. He got emphysema while abroad. So they returned to Canada and never went back.

Because of our parents' limited fun and travel, Marilyn and I vowed the same wouldn't happen to us if we could prevent it.

So we went to places, lots of places, and when the kids were older, they came along too and still do. As a result of our travels, which admittedly have been first class most of the time, we are often asked about our favourite destinations and hotels.

Here are a few hotels we'd happily visit tomorrow. Be warned: take plenty of money.

In no particular order: the Oriental in Bangkok; the Inn on the Park (Four Seasons) in London, thanks partly to its manager Ramon Pajares; the Hassler Hotel in Rome with its view of St. Peter's and the Spanish Steps; the Pierre in New York where George Schwab, now retired, was a world class manager; the San Domenico outside of Taormina, Sicily, an old monastery; the Cipriani in Venice, perhaps our favourite; the Hotel Palumbo in Ravello, Italy; Inverlochy Castle in northern Scotland, owned by a Canadian; Jasper Park Lodge in Alberta, Canada; (I could be convicted of a slight conflict of interest here. I worked as a caddy for a couple of summers and caddied for Bing Crosby when he won the Totem Pole tournament. Maybe the happiest summer of my young life.);

Horsted Place, seventy miles from London, a stately home with a Jack Nicklaus golf course in the back yard; the Amandari in Phuket, Thailand.

Gordon and Cathy Richardson are close pals of ours. Cathy is my favourite, since in a slightly earlier era she was Miss Toronto. She and Gordon were in Italy a few years ago staying near Positano where Gordon received the "bargain of a lifetime." His bill was $3,000 for the week which included three meals a day plus a chauffeur-driven car for seven days.

Gordon recommended the place to several friends as a wonderful buy as well as a great spot right on the ocean. His views changed dramatically two weeks after they returned home when he got the real bill. The first bill was only for the car.

The hotel he had been so happily recommending was the San Pietro which several of our friends claim is the best hotel in the world.

All of this leads handily to the sometimes controversial subject of Sun seminars, during which we try to make a little exotic travel available to some Sun staff. Each year the Sun Corporation takes the board, some senior staff and key employees and their spouses from all divisions for a four-day (or in some years a full week) visit somewhere. Our board always attends, and then complains that it is too expensive.

Let me explain my position. The Sun started with sixty-two people from the Telegram. Almost without exception, they came on board to the Sun where they worked harder and had more authority than they had before. Their salaries remained the same.

I felt we had to offer a future to them if we succeeded. And we did fairly well through the gifts of stock. That made them owners and, for sure, more responsible with their expense budgets than they might have been.

We offered three weeks of vacation after one year and kept upping it until the tenth year, when everyone was guaranteed an eight-week sabbatical with pay. The sabbatical would be repeated every ten years. It was likely one of the best things we did for our employees.

Many staffers began saving and planning four and five years ahead of their scheduled sabbaticals, and in many cases took trips which would have been way out of their reach until retirement. The sabbaticals are now in their second round, since the Sun has celebrated its twentieth anniversary.

When we started the *Toronto Sun*, we put in a holiday in February, just because February doesn't have one. We called it Blah Day and the employees worked out which day they wanted with their department head. Later we added a President's Day, a day off to be taken anytime during the year.

We insisted department heads put a small bonus fund in their annual budget so they could hand out bonuses constantly for work well done.

Each year, up until I left, I wrote each Sun employee describing how he or she was doing in relation to salary, pension accumulation and other benefits. I told them in some detail how each division of the company was doing and tried, as best I could, to talk about future plans.

When we wanted to keep people with the Sun, perhaps in the face of a job offer elsewhere, and didn't have the cash in hand for a competitive salary bid, we would sometimes slip him or her a car.

This was slightly abused and the new management, I

understand, is taking a lot of them back at the end of their leases.

Then there were the seminars. They were organized as a reward for employees we felt had earned a special place in the Sun, if you'll pardon the expression.

The seminars served a lot of purposes, not the least of which was simply to let the employees get to know each other, the directors, and their counterparts in the other Sun-owned operations. I always felt that they were in large part responsible for the family feeling that Sun staffers like to talk about.

We held half-day meetings consisting of publishers' reports and staff presentations. Moneyman Bruce Jackson and I would give the overview for the company. Then we'd have guest speakers from our suppliers, as well as celebrities. In the afternoons and evenings we'd play.

But the highlight of each seminar, at least for me, was the presentations by the staff from all divisions. We would schedule about twenty each year.

Everyone in the company, I'm sure, knew who attended each year and what they had done to earn it. And everyone knew he or she had a chance to earn a seminar invitation in the future. So I know of no animosity.

As the company grew, so did the seminars and, of course, their cost. In Sarasota, Florida, we had over 100 people at a total cost of about $400,000. I thought it was worthwhile for the company even at twice the price.

But I knew some of the directors were concerned, and properly so. We had planned a big bash in Hong Kong for our twentieth anniversary. After a lot of bottom-line watching and agonizing, I decided not to have it. I wrote everyone who had been invited letters of apology and thought I'd done it without too many problems.

The following year, we booked a small cruise ship in the Mediterranean to accommodate about 100 guests. The trip would take a week and, within reason, we could sail where we wanted to.

I didn't want to go two years without a seminar, but as we prepared to send invitations, I thought I'd talk to a few directors and see what they thought.

To be fair, they were concerned but would go along. I talked to Schipper, Solway, Cohon and Bratty and got that feeling. I talked differently to Ron Osborne at Maclean Hunter. I said I knew he was going through the same economic problems, so if a seminar would work against him, I'd cancel it.

He made it quite clear he didn't think we should be doing it, although he seemed fully aware of the up side. He said it wasn't his place to cancel it and that he would go if asked. I said that on that basis, I would go ahead and send out the invitations. I did. Marilyn and I then disappeared to Hong Kong and Bali on our second sabbatical.

Lionel Schipper caught up with me in New Zealand, or I should say, his fax machine did. It inferred at length that the board was concerned about the perception of holding the planned seminar in this economy. I had told some of them earlier this was not a huge concern of mine, but I didn't feel I could make my case very well from New Zealand.

I telephoned Paul Godfrey and told him to cancel the seminar. I told him to be very careful how he did it because I didn't want him blamed. To be honest, I was furious. I had asked these guys first, but then they'd changed their minds when I was out of town. I thought it was lousy. Anyway, we would have no seminar cruise that year.

After my return from my sabbatical, and with board approval, we starting planning a seminar in Hawaii. I'm glad we held off sending out the invitations, because we abandoned it also.

Last year we planned a seminar in California for March of 1993. Well, I got ousted before it happened and Godfrey hosted it. I'm betting it will be the last Sun seminar. We'll see.

Over the years our seminars took us to Niagara-on-the-Lake, Banff, Quebec City, Bermuda, London, England (twice), San Francisco, Calgary, New York, Houston, Washington, a Caribbean cruise, Jerusalem and Sarasota.

Our celebrity speakers included Premier Ralph Klein, mayor of Calgary; Ken Taylor, the Canadian hero from Iran; Helen Thomas, chief White House correspondent for UPI; Senator Phil Gramm from Texas, co-author of the Graham-Rudman legislation; Conrad Black; Barbara Amiel; Prime Minister Yitzak Shamir; and too many more to name.

The seminar became a unique and valuable Sun institution. It was a good management tool, a wonderful morale booster and a great deal of fun. I would certainly vote to continue with them,but then I don't have a vote anymore.

While we tried in the Sun's early days to avoid operational charts, focus groups and surveys, it was impossible to fight them off forever. Paul Godfrey was a fan. He could draw who-reports-to-whom charts on the back of any notebook.

We may have been casual, but I think we knew what was going on and could react quickly.

In 1990, the Sun made it into a book about the best 100 companies in Canada to work for. Certainly, the fact that our parent, Maclean Hunter, published the book had nothing to do with it.

Over the years, I developed a list of my own guidelines for a good newspaper put out by good people. For what they might be worth, here are some of those I've emphasized over the years to the staff.

1. There is no such thing as acceptable. Quality in service and delivery can always be better.

2. Quality is everyone's responsibility, from the corner office on the executive floor, to the people in the field. Reward results, not style.

3. Keep your ears and your mind open. Some of the best ideas come from unexpected sources. No one can do the job as well as we can, of course. But while it's easier to think we are always right, just occasionally someone may have a better way.

4. Develop detailed implementation plans. Just talking isn't enough. When you're writing the plan use "we" which is infinitely better than the self-serving "I."

Partnership is another word to take seriously. It implies equality in the conducting of business as well as shared participation in the rewards. Sun employees are shareholders and also participate in the profits.

5. Work together with other departments. Territorial imperatives are enor-

Tight Squeeze

Asked at a financial analysts lunch if I really needed a car and driver, I said: "Yes, definitely. But you must remember the early days. Marilyn and I had a compact car with room for Marilyn and me in the front and a picture of the kids in the back."

mous obstacles. If you don't know what they're up to in editorial, ask. If there is a problem in your own department, state it calmly and candidly. Then be patient and listen for a possible solution other than yours. Don't be afraid to say "I don't know." Also, be on time for meetings and, just as importantly, make them end on time.

6. Make extraordinary efforts in unusual situations and keep the subscriber aware. They will remember you appreciatively when you get their newspaper to them in a snowstorm or take the trouble to explain why you couldn't.

7. Tell people that they are doing a good job when they are and reward them accordingly. Our business has become more transient and we must pay regular attention to the physical environment people have to work in if we are to keep them around and happy.

8. Have senior management visible and accessible. Talk often to employees, but don't be a drone. Have fun in your job.

9. Most importantly, at the Sun we want our senior people to be terrific leaders. Terrific leaders usually have terrific teams.

10. Recognize that the best work is done by individuals placed in the right job for their capabilities. You can search the parks and public buildings in the four cities in which we publish Suns without finding a statue to a committee.

In the end, the Sun turned out to be a case study of entrepreneurship and risk. We ran the gamut together, the directors, employees, readers, advertisers and me. We tasted triumph and disaster. We won big and lost our share as well. We saw bad times and good times, and even some great times.

I like to think we represented our readers to the point that we're now part of the texture of life in Toronto.

We did it on gut feel. We rode the roller coaster and made some calls by the feeling in the pit of our stomach. We trusted ourselves to know the right path.

That path, I figured, included the third of our population who are avid sports fans and readers of a good sports section. We had that from day one.

I knew we were in the age of baby boomers who were becoming all-powerful in our world. Generally speaking, we thought that besides sports, they loved to travel and be entertained.

Therefore, we've run since almost day one a Sun travel section, which appears twice a week — Wednesdays and Sundays. We've been providing major entertainment coverage with a young, active staff, led initially by George Anthony, who now runs CBC entertainment.

The fact is, there is a noticeable trend toward decreasing readership of newspapers. I think that the trend can be reversed by good old-fashioned newspapering and a little attention to the wishes of newspaper readers.

Nonetheless, in 1991, I was dragged kicking and screaming into letting some of the staff experiment with surveys, focus groups and more scientific measurement schemes.

I've always been very negative about this sort of testing of the waters. My visions were of little people brandishing charts, graphics and computer printouts. They would have no idea what the editorial people did. Nor would their computer printouts tell them. They wouldn't understand that a writer staring out the window might actually be working. My fear was, and is, that given free rein to do what they wanted, they would create for us a Wizard of Oz newspaper — one with no heart, no brain and no courage. A newspaper cannot be any better than the newspaper men and women who put it out.

Quite often now, I feel that simple things that worked are becoming complicated again.

Virtually every newspaper in North America is losing circulation due to major price hikes and the influence of television. What we don't need now is to hold six meetings, write twelve reports, throw in a focus group or two, and then do nothing.

The best thing newspaper managers could do now would be to make a huge bonfire out of all the office and meeting room doors.

We need once again to start taking our newspapers and our readers seriously. Not ourselves.

Graham Leggat is one immigrant liked by everyone. He was lured to Canada to help make soccer big time in Canada. It wasn't his fault it never happened.

Although he still broadcasts some soccer, his main chore is now public relations and public speaking. Since the day the Sun started, I had a copy of the Sun delivered to every early-morning disc jockey and to each of their newsrooms. It contained what they wanted — short stories, some valuable one-liners, a story or two to scalp, and a Sunshine Girl to like or dislike. It was good cheap publicity for the paper. Graham knew that and used it. The first time he introduced me at a speaking engagement, he speculated on who read some of the newspapers in Canada:

"The *Globe and Mail*," he said "is read by people who think they are running the country but aren't.

"The *Toronto Star* is read by people who know they should be running the country, but aren't.

"The *Ottawa Citizen* is read by people who are running the country and don't know how to.

"And the Sun is read by people who don't give a damn who's running the country, as long as she has big boobs."

He got such a laugh out of that he tried again the next time we were at the head table.

This time he wondered how the Toronto papers would cover the sinking of the Titanic if it happened today.

The Globe, he felt, would run the story in the shipping section of the *Report on Business* with the heading: "Cargo Lost at Sea."

The Star would announce: "Star Reporter Saves Dog as Hundreds Drown."

The Sun would say: "Crew Members Demand Sex Before Women Allowed in Lifeboats. Guess the Death Toll. New Sun Contest. Page 63."

CHAPTER 14

All-Stars

We had just finished preparing the budgets that would guide us through 1993 when the axe fell on me. As part of that process we had tried, as we do every year, to look into the future, to see what lay ahead for the Sun and for newspapers in general. The future, as usual, was murky, and destined to be, as it always is, a crap shoot.

Times have not been good for newspapers so far in this decade. Only phenomenally large discounts from newsprint suppliers in recent years have kept most newspapers in the black.

But there is some evidence those discounts are ending — although not immediately. Newsprint supplies have stabilized, and a lot of production has been stopped. The price increases will hit us as soon as they can be safely implemented.

Meanwhile, advertising lineage in Canada has remained flat or even down from previous years. There is some indication in parts of the U.S. that a recovery has started.

Virtually every major newspaper in North America is losing circulation. The industry has raised delivery prices fairly dramatically in an unsettled economy, triggering the accompanying drop in circulation.

Personally, I think television poses the major threat to newspapers. The printed word is losing the fight with television for the hearts and minds of the news junkie. Television's improved graphic technology and longer news shows are beginning to contain information of substance. Television can actually bring a war, as it happens, into your living room. Newspapers can't keep up. The days of the scoop, except by investigative reporters, are gone.

Nonetheless, all of that does not necessarily signal our demise. It is not generally known that when a major story breaks on the tube, newspaper sales increase the next day. Our worry is the average day, when morning and evening television news eats into what used to be newspaper-reading time.

Many in our business despair for our future, especially a future for journalists. I don't think the situation is life-threatening unless we collectively panic.

I remember watching "the first" television newspaper on a screen in the British Air lounge at Heathrow. We were told it was the first step on the way to the electronic newspaper which would lead ultimately to the death of newspapers.

Now it's long gone.

I know we must look ahead so as not to fall behind. I know we are past the beginning of a media revolution that is changing the role for newspapers. We are in a battle to hold our market share and remain the principal provider of news.

I know the rapid technological developments will create new roles for tomorrow's editors.

But I also know that a newspaper can only be as good as

the editorial product the newspaper men and women put out. The same is true for a television news show. Good journalists will survive and flourish.

Now is the time for leaders with nerves of steel. The times in which we live will test every company. But as they say, for every pitfall, there is an opportunity.

Our leaders must remain calm and courageous, so as to be able to pluck the opportunities from amongst the pitfalls and tell the difference between the two.

I once asked Hartley Steward in the early days of the Sun if he really thought it necessary that we make every mistake on our way to the perfect tabloid newspaper. I said it in jest of course, but the fact is we were in uncharted waters and we were bound to make our fair share of mistakes.

Much has been made of our unique experience, and I've been asked many times how we did it and what we would do differently given a chance to do it all over again.

On the assumption that we can learn from others' mistakes, here is what I would do the second time around:

• I would watch bad debts constantly and make sure that I knew the credit manager well enough so that he'd let me know about every major problem before it became a catastrophe.

In 1976, I wrote Don Hunt a memo saying "you may note with sorrow or anger that the Sun has the worst record in Canada for bad debts with an average of 102 days. The best is thirty-seven days, and the Star is at forty-seven days."

Soon after that we found a guy named Peter Kotzer who took one look at our debts outstanding and went to work. We will never be last again, or even close, as long as we have

Peter Kotzer managing our collections and credit.

• I would not let any of my staff commit to purchasing newsprint alone. It is such a volatile world and so labour- oriented that two senior people should sign each contract.

• I would get a daily report on the newshole and advertising space planned for the next day's paper.

• I would continue our sabbatical and seminar programs. Weighted against the cost of being unionized, it's money well spent.

• I would throw out every survey-taker, especially the ones who guarantee to improve morale while spending less money.

When I moved Paul Godfrey to the position of president and chief operating officer, he naturally had to be replaced as publisher. I tried several times to convince Paul that publisher of the *Toronto Sun* was the best job in the corporation. He quite frankly said his ego wouldn't let him not want to be president. I made the appointment.

He recommended Jim Tighe as publisher. My first choice was Hartley Steward, who said he preferred Ottawa, at that time anyway. After a while I agreed with Godfrey's choice. Paul and I discussed this fully and we shared our doubts. We agreed first of all that Tighe was a terrific guy and popular with those who worked for him. We hoped he could make the hard decisions and in the end we decided he was the best equipped for the job.

The next choice was not quite as democratic. I insisted that the general manager in Toronto should be Wayne Parrish, who at the time was my assistant in charge of editorial. Godfrey disagreed. I took Tighe to lunch, and he agreed with

Godfrey. We then held a vote, which I won with my one vote. Parrish would be general manager. I was determined we have an editorial voice in the hierarchy.

To say that Parrish was surprised is putting it mildly, but he adjusted.

I had had an earlier dinner meeting with Wayne and agreed that as part of his responsibilities, he would be allowed to "clean-up" the paper. By clean-up I meant making the typeface standard throughout the paper, plus any number of other housekeeping measures to make the paper consistent in its appearance from back to front. Department heads like to inject themselves and their creative bent into "their" pages, not understanding, sometimes, that they are really "our" pages. Wayne's view of a clean-up was vastly different from mine.

He freed up two young editors for the project, alienating older editors who had more authority. They set to work and, months later, their clean-up touched almost every page.

The clean-up was headed for a dust-up.

As I was sitting proudly in the new $46 million addition to our building, I found out that Parrish had rented space off-site so his whiz kids wouldn't be disturbed — or seen maybe. I told him to put them back in the office before I firebombed their place.

A couple of directors asked me if I was yelling in my office during afternoon meetings with Parrish. I yelled: "You're goddamned right I am!"

I still do occasionally when I'm all alone and can't find the sports section on Saturday. We built the daily as a one-section paper. Now you have to find the life section and get rid of the classified advertising section before you can find sports.

Fifty percent of our daily sales comes from boxes, the other fifty percent from newsstands. Thus, in my view, the front page is critical. The page represents our instant response to readers' interests as he or she walks towards one of our boxes.

Bear in mind that the story we are featuring has generally been shown on television or heard on the radio before our paper hits the street. This is one reason newspapers are changing and must change. Television news has removed the filter of time between the event and when we hear about it.

◆ ◆ ◆

My view from the beginning of the Sun was that we had to analyse and opinionate on the news. We needed lots of columns written by strong columnists.

While I wanted to keep a one-section paper, Parrish seemed to want as many as the presses could accommodate.

All of which is to say that if I had it all to do over again I might have kept a closer reign on my friend Wayne Parrish. This is not to say that I have changed my mind on Wayne. I still think that he is one of the Sun's bright lights and, who knows, maybe he was right.

I have always argued that only a very few columnists have readers who would follow them to another paper.

My hope at the Sun was to try to detect young writers with a future, and aim them at a columnist-style of writing. From time to time I thought I'd done well in this area.

The most sustained circulation growth we had, I think, was when a reader could turn the page twice and be exposed to the Sunshine Girl, Paul Rimstead and Gary Dunford. This wasn't highbrow stuff, but it was a powerful one-two-three punch for a morning tabloid. A serendipitous kick-start to the day. Toronto loved all three.

Right now I think Christie Blatchford is a wonderful addition to the front five pages of the *Toronto Sun*. She can add her insights to any story without duplicating the efforts of other staffers assigned to the same thing. During the splendid performance of the Toronto Maple Leafs in the recent hockey playoffs, I read Christie regularly. She was also splendid.

Peter Worthington was and is a reader-grabber. In the early *Toronto Sun* days, we received more letters to the editor than the Telegram was receiving after eighty-seven years. In those days Worthington wrote almost every editorial, as well as his bylined column. The annual readership survey, which we did strictly through the paper,

Lancelot

Newspapers hire many free-lancers. Where did the word come from? From the Middle Ages when knights without an overlord rented their lances (and themselves) to other over-lords and fought their battles.

showed the editorial pages were read by almost every reader who picked up a Sun. Worthington, as well as the lovely and beautiful Barbara Amiel who followed him, gave a special something to those pages.

As we got bigger, I think we got blander. As far as the columnists writing on the editorial pages go, they continue to get older. Significantly, I don't see any fresh young faces peering over the shoulders of the veterans.

Allan Fotheringham, though certainly not a fresh young face, is probably the best-read columnist in Canada. Eric Margolis, too, has found a niche for himself and continues to grow in popularity. A comer is Lorrie Goldstein who, to my mind, could write more.

Jim O'Leary in London and Steve Simmons in sports are

usually special reads for me. So was Wayne Parrish when he did the sports columns.

Paul Stanway, executive editor in Edmonton, is another one of my favourites, as is Mark Bonokoski, the editor in Ottawa.

Bob Pennington, who passed away a few years ago, is very much missed.

Donato's cartoons, of course, round out the op-ed pages, as we call the more analytical and insightful pages which usually appear opposite the editorial page. In twenty-one years I only killed two of Donato's cartoons. He was furious, naturally, but emerged victorious anyway. He sold them as special collector's items at a charitable auction for $1,000 each.

Andy loves golf but should stick to cartooning.

Once, when the paper was filled with news on organized crime, he drew a cartoon of a vile-looking mafia type with cigars, guns and wire sticking out of his pockets. Sun director Rudy Bratty phoned me early in the morning to say he was resigning from the board because, "Donato has done an insulting drawing of my dad."

I said: "Rudy, your dad's dead. How would Andy even know what he looks like?"

To my surprise, two other prominent Italians thought he'd drawn them and had their lawyers call.

I set up a lunch at Winston's with all concerned. Nobody looked like anybody else and certainly nobody looked like the character in Donato's cartoon. We had a couple of bottles of wine and left amicably.

From my vantage point in retirement I watch anxiously to see what will happen in the world of Sun columnists in the future. Whatever happens, we've learned that columnists are vital to the success of newspapers like the Sun.

Where Would I Be
Without Them?

I t's true that I don't trust surveys. But I recently read one
that interested me. This survey listed the most common
complaints secretaries have about their bosses.

The top three unfavourite bosses are those who keep
their secretaries on overtime without previous notice; those
who dawdle until quitting time and then decide to do dicta-
tion; and those who hover over their secretaries while they
type, pointing out errors.

Guilty! I am guilty on all three charges.

It's simple to buy a person's time, but it's impossible to
buy their enthusiasm and loyalty. You must earn those.

Somehow, where my secretaries were concerned, I did. All
of them were tremendous. I couldn't have functioned without them.

I viewed them as equals who were perfectly free to say
what they felt, and they did. I said earlier that my forced early
retirement affected far more people than my family and the
board.

Certainly it affected deeply the lives of Lynn Carpenter,
my executive assistant, and Annemarie Cimowsky, my assistant. I don't like the title "secretary."

The three of us now have offices in downtown Toronto under an eighteen-month arrangement with the Sun. The girls are guaranteed jobs back at the Sun, although they will certainly not be the same as those they performed for me.

Although we do our best not to mention it, I think the three of us are bored and miss the action. Whatever the outcome of all this, I can't thank them enough. They have been friends, not employees.

◆ ◆ ◆

My first secretary when I became sports editor at the Tely was Jenny Wingerson, a pretty Canadian Olympic hurdler.

In those days, the paper sponsored the Indoor Games, a giant track meet at Maple Leaf Gardens. Tickets weren't moving very quickly so we decided to promote the event a little.

I asked Jenny to jump over a few tables in the staff cafeteria and we'd run a silhouette picture. The next day when I went to the composing room, an employee in the art department stopped me to say Jenny was "fooling around" with her picture.

"What do you mean?" I asked.

"She's making her chest bigger," he said.

"What does it look like?" I asked.

"Better," he said.

"Then let's run it," I told him.

Shortly after Lynn joined me as my assistant at the Sun, there was a board meeting in Calgary. We arrived late and were rushing. Lynn opened her hotel room door to find a guy in her bed. She beat a hasty retreat.

A few hours later, after the meeting ended, Lynn tried it again. This time the room was empty, but straight ahead of her was a big double bed — empty — but turned down on both sides. Lynn suspected the worst but, of course, it was just the maid.

Lynn learned fast however, organizing some great seminars for us before handing the responsibilities over to Annemarie.

Annemarie's first solo effort was taking 100 of us to Israel. We had then Prime Minister Yitzak Shamir as a guest speaker, along with the mayors of Tel Aviv and Jerusalem and the Canadian ambassador.

We never did have a bad seminar, but I think Annemarie's were more difficult to organize, perhaps because we were travelling further away than we had in the past.

I doubt there is anyone in the city better at organizing these things. However, she says that that part of her career is over for now. Too bad.

Ann Rankin, a lovely Scottish girl, was my first secretary at the Sun. We pulled one age-old newspaper trick on her which worked, but she never fell for anything else.

I sent her to the city desk for a package of rubber nails. The city editor was well briefed and sent her to composing. They'd run out of course. She tried two more departments as she moved towards panic stations.

I happened to look out the window and saw Ann walking along King Street. I thought, my God, she's quitting. I found her in a hardware store a few blocks away trying to explain to a laughing clerk that this was her first assignment and she would fail unless he could help.

I felt so bad that I was going to get someone to make me a package of rubber nails.

This brings me to Trudy Eagan.

◆ ◆ ◆

When I decided to write a book a few years ago, I visualized it as a happy leap from the defunct Telegram to the successes of the Sun. In twenty years, we'd provided employment for over 2,000 people. We'd had our peaks and valleys, but we were making money and we had very little debt.

I had never for a moment feared being pushed out by my own company. That's why I find it extremely difficult to write about those of "my friends" who played a role I still don't understand.

I wanted to write a collection of memories, not an assessment of my stewardship. Unfortunately, in part I find myself doing the latter too often.

"Why not simply leave them out of the book?" someone suggested. But I couldn't leave Trudy Eagan Peddie out of any book involving the Sun.

It was not long after she joined me that I realized she made the people she dealt with discover a little more pleasure in themselves.

In the early days and for many years afterwards, practically anyone who had a problem went to Trudy and came away at least pacified. You can't measure, or even discover all she contributed, but it was a lot, and greatly appreciated.

I remember a dinner with her at the Harbour Castle Hotel when I told her she could become a department head and then, I hoped, graduate to the board of directors. I remember telling her that it meant she and I would not share all the information we were used to sharing. That function would now be done by Lynn Carpenter. I wonder, in retrospect, if that bothered her.

I don't know when I realized I was beginning to lose her, but it was shortly after Paul Godfrey joined us. I thought, too, that her temperament changed. But I knew Godfrey was on his way up and thought he needed someone he could consult with. Also, I was getting ready to write a book in my retirement.

I understood why the board never involved her in its initial discussions and the decision involving my departure. Still, surely a director is a director all the time.

I will never understand why Trudy (and Paul) didn't stand up and say: "Wait a minute. Where's Doug? What has he got to say? He hired me, promoted me, put me on the board and you guys think I should sit here and say nothing? Well I won't."

All that I heard from that board meeting was a loud silence. A unanimous decision, they told me.

I was, and am, more sad than mad. I will not speak publicly to the board because I don't want them to be able to say we're mending our fences. We are not.

I told Ron Osborne at the time that there would be a lot of personal damage incurred by the board's decision. This is a classic case of it. It's the kind of hurt that never ends.

CHAPTER 16

The Golden-Age Gang

I was talking to Jean Charest at lunch just before the Conservative leadership race. His campaign, mounted too late, left him a close second. He noticed that I didn't seem to be paying attention to what he was saying. I apologized and said: "I'm sorry, it just occurred to me that you're two years younger than my middle son, Bruce."

I have no particular aversion to a thirty-four-year-old running our country. Lord knows he couldn't do worse than some we've had in the past few decades.

However, it does seem to me that we have a tendency to toss the aging out and replace them with youth with no experience. Surely we should be able to find a formula that gives us the best of both worlds.

I started thinking about this twenty-one years ago when I went to Russia for the hockey series with Lorne Duguid and Jack Callen.

Duguid was a former NHL star who had become executive V.P. of a liquor company once he retired from hockey. One of Duguid's first assignments had been to write the rules requiring senior officers and board members to retire at seventy. Now, at seventy, he was trying to find a way around them.

Callen, the senior Air Canada man in Toronto, was for some mystifying reason given two years' salary to retire two years early. How the hell anyone in Air Canada could justify this as good business is beyond me. He was one of the best they had.

Anyway, in a rush they were gone. I have no idea if retirement had anything to do with it, but both died within a few years. But when they were working they were vibrant, quick-thinking individuals and good friends, who I still miss today.

With my corporate demise, I've time to look around and look back. I can think of some retirements, willing and not-so-willing, that just should not have been. This applies to both the people and the organizations involved.

I guess it has a little to do with my age, but they seem to be breaking up, that old gang of mine. My Golden Age Gang. Could we live to rule again? Not likely, but we dream.

Pierre Trudeau retired as prime minister twice. A year or two after the second time, Marilyn and I saw him in action in New York at a party Bob Campeau was throwing to honour himself at the Metropolitan Museum of Art.

Trudeau arrived with Margot Kidder (Lois Lane in the movie *Superman*). They both looked sensational, but unfortunately, they weren't sitting together. The former P.M. soon looked after that.

He was sitting between Mrs. Campeau and the wife of the president of First Boston Bank. Margot was sitting next to Cardinal Carter. Trudeau somehow got the band playing about two hours before it was supposed to.

He leapt to his feet and asked Margot to dance. The others at the table, except the Cardinal, although surprised, also got up.

As soon as they were on the dance floor, Pierre whistled back and traded place cards. The Cardinal found himself with the president of First Boston's wife at his side, while across the table was Trudeau with his arms around Margot. On top of that they left early.

I thought, how could I have voted against that guy? He's in my gang if he wants to be.

Marilyn and I witnessed the show from another table. We were sitting with Paddy Ann and Latham Burns. Latham was then chairman of Burns Fry. He is now honourary chairman with no executive role. Fortunately, he has an office at Burns Fry and his partners have the good sense to ask his advice. Latham likes tennis, swimming, reading, good drink, good food and Paddy Ann, who is younger.

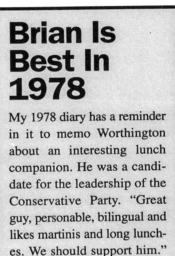

Brian Is Best In 1978

My 1978 diary has a reminder in it to memo Worthington about an interesting lunch companion. He was a candidate for the leadership of the Conservative Party. "Great guy, personable, bilingual and likes martinis and long lunches. We should support him." He was Brian Mulroney.

It doesn't read like a case for retirement to anyone who knows him.

Peter Worthington, a founder of the Sun, is also eligible for our little group, having resigned or been fired (by me) any number of times. (Neither of us is sure how many since both happened several times.) He'll write "Our Reasons Why" again, as he did in 1971 for the Sun. It will be much more succinct and readable than the current Sun's thirty-word mission statement, written by about thirteen people over two days of meetings.

The Sun has a regulation forcing directors to retire at seventy. It was spearheaded by Don Campbell of Maclean Hunter, who has two years still to go. The board, including me, voted unanimously for this. We never thought anything more about it until our time came.

We've lost three directors so far to this rule. I made a speech in their honour at our annual meeting two years ago.

It applied to John Grant, Jim McCallum and Fred Metcalfe who I thought and still think were three of our best directors, although I'm souring a bit on Fred, I must admit. I kept sending him reports and invitations to the seminars — the same material I sent to the rest of the board. When the axe fell on me, Fred never wrote or called. I guess it was a victory for Maclean Hunter over friendship.

I never felt that seventy was a milestone after which one automatically lost one's ability to help a company. What I felt was that twenty years was longer than anyone should lead a company. But I must admit I never wanted to go beyond talking about it.

I think my first friend subjected to retirement was Lorne

Johnny, Can You Spare a Dime?

Conrad Black and I boycotted Winston's for several weeks because we thought proprietor John Arena had leaked information on us to Peter Newman. We returned triumphantly amidst a lot of bowing and scraping.

Later the parking lot attendant wanted ten dollars. Conrad and I between us didn't have it. We had to borrow it from Arena.

Lodge, who was retired by IBM as its leader in Canada. Lorne wasn't seventy, not even sixty. He had only recently celebrated living past fifty, an age at which most Lodges died, Lorne said.

I'll never forget playing golf with Lorne in Florida when he was dragged off the course by a call from Ken Thomson. Ken, who was on the IBM board when the reluctant retirement happened, was horribly upset and thought the method used was abominable. He wanted to tell Lorne how he felt and that he had personally called IBM to insist they publish his letter praising Lorne in their monthly report to employees.

Sometimes you hear anti-Thomson stories. This certainly isn't one of them.

IBM, to be fair, said Lorne headed their Canadian operation for fourteen years, longer than anyone else in Canada. Fair ball, but still a little insensitive.

The rest of our gang started sinking like stones.

Fraser Elliott, senior partner of his large law firm, didn't want to give up the chairmanship of CAE at seventy. He hung on for one more year, then gave it up to become a director.

But why the hell not. He'd only been chairman for thirty-six years, and owns the most shares, and is as sharp as a knife.

Other contenders for my club are Bill Heaslip, president of the Grafton Group, which he had worked for since he graduated from Humberside Collegiate; Gordon Gray, retired from Royal LePage; and Martin Emmett, axed by Tambrands. Every once in a while I also see Len Lumbers from Bell drinking martinis at the York Club and plotting impossible takeovers. Wouldn't it be fun to have them all together on one board?

It seems the theory is that the way to live longer is to cut off all the things that made you want to live longer.

Just after I got the axe, my great friend, Peter Eby, bit the
dust temporarily. He keeled over from a heart attack in the
Regency bar in New York — a single malt scotch in hand.
Fortunately Martin Emmett was with him, because when Pete
recovered consciousness, he insisted on being taken to his
room. Marty made him go to the hospital where he promptly
had two more attacks. He is now on the way to a full recovery,
but I think we've seen the end of a certain lifestyle.

I'm glad it's me writing about Eby. He's the vice-chairman
of Burns Fry and the Sun's financial advisor for many years,

P.M. Meets Heineken

Joe Clark was the first prime minister to come to the Sun. He was
arriving at 11:00 a.m. for a tour, a meeting with our editorial board
and lunch, which we had no room to serve him in our building.

Joe and his wife had recently received some bad publicity because
they had taken cases of Heineken beer with them on an official trip
to Japan. Much to the anger of the Canadian brewers, Joe described
it as his favourite beer.

We took him to the Albany Club for lunch.

The waiter was leaving as we arrived.

"Where the hell are you going?" I asked.

"Downstairs to get a Heineken for the P.M.," the waiter said.

"You can't leave," I said. "You're the only staff guy serving." I
asked him what kind of beer he had.

"Labatts Blue," the waiter said.

"Fill up the glasses and give them to me," I said.

I carried the two glasses of beer into Joe and said buoyantly:
"Where did you get to like Heineken, Prime Minister? It's my
favourite beer too!"

We sipped away. I agreed with Joe that Heineken was a "distinc-
tive, yet lighter taste worth paying more for."

as well as being a great friend.

I know all there is to know about him, and I think I have the good sense not to tell it all.

He is among the top ten knee dancers in the world (there are only fourteen), and he won the Nightingale Cup from Berkeley Square for non-stop dancing in Annabel's in 1987.

When Martin Emmett got turfed out by his board, I left a message on his answering machine asking if he'd like to be vice-chairman of the Golden Age Gang I was thinking of forming.

Then I thought we'd add Cardinal Carter, another non-retiring retiree. He was at the party John Turner and I threw for John Arena at Winston's.

His Eminence has trouble with his walking after a stroke a few years ago. He needed help to get to the first landing, so we sat him there to sip on a martini (maybe two) and greet his old buddies as they came in.

When dinner was called, the Cardinal stood up and marched up the second set of steps unaided. When I stood up to welcome everyone, I mentioned the Cardinal's climb and said I wasn't sure whether I was at Winston's or Lourdes.

We'll all be at the formative meeting at the 21 Club in New York in October. If you've got a company that needs a board, come on down. We'll buy you a drink, and maybe you can get blessed. A duplicate of your pension cheque or birth certificate would be all you need to get in. We'll be the guys with the white hair or no hair.

We'll be delighted to see you.

CHAPTER 17

Eclipsed

There comes a moment in most of our lives when we are overwhelmed by our inability to understand what has happened to us.

My moment came on November 27, 1992, on my sixty-fourth birthday, which I was not planning to celebrate.

Running a company for twenty years can be tiring. So can turning sixty-four. My wife started comparing me to our old television set. Your colour starts to fade, you take longer to warm up, your instant on is off and your vertical hold starts to go.

That bewildering day most of the Sun staff — about 900 of them — were jammed into the old Eclipse building where the Sun was first published.

They were chanting — "Doug! Doug! Doug!" — and trying to shake my hand or hug me as my family and I made our way to a makeshift platform.

I don't know enough superlatives to adequately write about this, the most emotional event in our lives. Marilyn and I were simply doing our best not to cry.

A series of wonderful columns had appeared in the Sun

before the party, and feelings were running high. The staff had originated the idea for this and paid for it themselves. I will never forget it. It was like reading and hearing your obituary without having to die.

A few weeks before the party, two directors — Herb Solway and Ron Osborne — "guided me out the door." They told me Paul Godfrey was going to succeed me as chief executive officer immediately.

My twenty-one-year love affair was over.

I telephoned my wife in her car and told her to pull over before I told her the news. "Drive home immediately," I said. "We're going away tonight."

I would not be at the Sun to stand with the directors when the announcement of my departure was made. I wanted it quite clear that they had taken control of the company without my agreement.

I also noted with interest that, of the "unanimous" board decision, only Ron Osborne and Lionel Schipper turned up to make the announcement to the Sun and *Financial Post* staff.

I know no one should manage beyond his time. The board and I obviously differed on when that was, although certainly Osborne and Campbell had agreed with me in our exchange of letters two months earlier.

The decision of the board seemed to me fairly simple. The word was out, they said, that I was souring on Paul Godfrey as my successor, and my departure was the only thing they could do to ensure Paul got the top Sun job.

This is mostly conjecture on my part because, mystifying as it is, none of the board talked to me about the issue until that D-Day. Surely it was a strange way to treat a founder and CEO.

Inexplicable to me was the behaviour of my good friends

Rudy Bratty and George Cohon. Their votes against me and their silence afterwards have tragically, for Marilyn and me at least, ended two relationships that we cherished.

The so-called antipathy between Paul Godfrey and myself was badly exaggerated in my view. Certainly we had strong disagreements over some budget issues, particularly involving the *Financial Post* and my refusal to lay off employees.

Paul is very sensitive to criticism. On the other hand, I've never done budgets without fighting with someone.

Paul and I had dinner the night before my ouster, after a budget session at Niagara-on-the-Lake. We both thought it was good that we had a chance to talk alone. It was quite a friendly repast but you could also call it our last supper.

At the budget meetings, I had made it very clear, and I thought Paul had agreed, that for the first time in our history the *Toronto Sun* was hurting. Besides battling the recession, we were losing a bit of market share.

I thought Paul agreed with this.

Henry Longfellow wrote: "He has achieved success who has lived well and laughed often."

To me that was the essence of our style over the years at the Sun. We worked hard, we played hard, we laughed often. The results were extraordinary. As a company we grew and expanded aggressively, all the while making solid profits. Now you see us, a large company almost debt-free. We started a company, nurtured it through its adolescence and turned it into a successful, mature corporation.

And for sure we laughed more than our share.

Even though the laughs have been minimal since the change of command, it is important that the company never lose its entrepreneurial spirit.

There is a preoccupation now with being leaner and meaner — to introduce every form of efficiency.

My stance was, and would be now, that savings were needed, certainly, but not necessarily without growth. And definitely no lay-offs, at least not at that time. I knew it was a position at odds with the board. What I didn't know was that the disagreement would be terminal.

Certainly a lot of companies are laying off staff. I think our organization is unique and very competitive. Every company must fight the recession in its own way. The Sun should remain entrepreneurial.

I know a lot of people have asked my former director friends why they did what they did to me. Most everyone says they have not had a satisfactory reply.

Through all the anguish, Marilyn, as well as our three boys and their wives, could not have been more loyal and supportive. I will never be able to thank them enough.

I should say here that for most of my twenty-one years at the Sun these were adjectives I applied to the board, and that I think the board applied to me.

One director, best unnamed, told me he realized many years ago I might be trouble. He was watching me coach a scrub baseball game. Ten of us had rented a cottage at Big Bay Point, north of Toronto, with the idea of playing every weekend in the annual fall fair ball tournament.

This tournament was in Creemore, a small town near Barrie. Since there were ten of us, we took turns being coach. In Creemore, I was it. We were in the top of the fourth (of a five-inning championship game), losing 3-0 to the home team which had a one-armed pitcher who definitely had our number.

I decided desperate measures were needed. I flashed the bunt sign to the first hitter in the fourth inning. He objected but did lay one down. The pitcher came off the mound and grabbed the ball, but had to turn around to throw. The ball went into right field, and our guy wound up on second. The next four bunted safely. The next guy cranked out a home run. Game over.

The crowd was furious. Considerable beer had been consumed and they were getting ugly.

Beating the one-armed baseball hero of Creemore was just not done. For the first time in my life I had a police escort out of town. For the aforementioned director that day marked me as a bad character.

I take pride in the fact I have been a journalist most of my life. Although I helped form a union at the old Telegram, I think the Sun has functioned better without unions.

Part of the reason for instituting seminars, sabbaticals, blah days and what some would term expensive parties and entertainment was to help keep us union-free.

This has led without doubt to a more efficient, successful and powerful operation. This newspaper has a great sense of itself and its purpose. It has a higher set of values and wields more influence than many might think

I like to think that I had a good rapport with our staff, and they with me. This led, from time to time, to splendid nights followed by great morning reads — and always arguments on how we could do better.

They were proud of being part of an organization which started out of the ashes of another newspaper. Most of us knew people who ran papers. Some of us had worked for John Bassett, who folded the Telegram, but none of us had ever heard of anyone who started a paper. We did, and it helped us forge a deeper, more involved relationship. We successfully produced our "daily miracle" and went on to do it again in Edmonton, Calgary, Ottawa and with the *Financial Post.*

The accountants and the lawyers never understood it. All they thought was that it cost too much.

May I recommend to our board the words of Napoleon Bonaparte in 1817. "Journalists are gamblers, grumblers and tutors of nations. Four hostile newspapers are more to be feared than a thousand bayonets," he said.

Napoleon, bless his heart, wasn't talking about circulation and advertising. He was talking about the product — how it read, how it looked, what it said.

The quality of the product is as vital now as it was in 1817. And a paper can never be any better than the reporters and editors who put it out.

It was those reporters and editors who had the great idea to stage my farewell party at the Eclipse building. It was like stepping back into my journalistic past.

On day one of the *Toronto Sun* there were sixty-two people in that building. On this day there were 900 chanting and applauding.

I stood in front of them and tried to speak.

"I was very mad, then very sad," I said. "The damage to my family has been much greater than I imagined it would be. It has been intolerable. How, in less than two months, did I become not a lame duck, but a dead duck?

"A couple of months ago I called this paper mine. It's not. It's yours," I said.

"No!" roared the great crowd. "It's yours."

"I'll settle for ours," I said and stepped way, drained completely.

I was with my real friends — the staff. I will never forget them. Nor will I forget that they were the real heroes who helped to create the company.

If I had to leave, it at least ended where it all began.